PITCHING STRATEGIES EXPLAINED

A PARENT'S GUIDE

DAN RUSSELL

Prior to beginning any exercise program, you must consult with your physician. You must also consult your physician before increasing the intensity of your training. The information in this book is intended for healthy individuals. Any application of the recommended material in this book is at the sole risk of the reader, and at the reader's discretion. Responsibility of any injuries or other adverse effects resulting from the application of any of the information provided within this book is expressly disclaimed.

Published by Price World Publishing
3971 Hoover Rd. Suite 77
Columbus, OH 43123-2839
www.PriceWorldPublishing.com

Cover Design by Russell Marleau
Layout Design by Merwin Loquias
Editing by Vanessa Fravel
Printing by Cushing-Malloy, Inc.

ISBN: 9781932549843
eISBN: 9781619842342
Library of Congress Control Number: 2013931809

Printed in the United States of America
10 9 8 7 6 5 4 3 2 1

For information about discounts for bulk purchases, please contact info@priceworldpublishing.com.

PITCHING STRATEGIES EXPLAINED

A PARENT'S GUIDE

DAN RUSSELL

TABLE OF CONTENTS

FOREWORD *7*

CHAPTER 1: *Pitching Strategies*
– Preliminaries And Principles *9*

CHAPTER 2: *Pitching Strategies*
– Tactics And Adjustments *59*

CHAPTER 3: *Holding Runners And Pickoff Moves*.............. *133*

CHAPTER 4: *Understanding The Batter*............................... *189*

CHAPTER 5: *The Emotional Game* *213*

FOREWORD

The marketplace is filled with books, many by former major league players, offering instruction on how to pitch. For the most part these books offer insights into how to stand, throw, pitch, and pick off base-runners. But surprisingly, there are too few books that help players who want to learn how to pitch that have anything at all to say about how pitchers should think.

And yet, thinking is a key element of every part of this game. Like chess, it has often been referred to as a thinking-man's game. Well, the purpose of this book is to offer these thinking insights to your son who must learn to grasp them if they are to become a successful pitcher.

I begin with describing some of the fundamental concepts about pitching that your son must understand. Then, pitching principles are described that will provide the pitching backbone to your son's in-game performance. Then, more specific strategies are offered as your son is required to make adjustments to the batters and situations in which he finds himself. But while your son is making adjustments, so are the batters. Chapter five provides your son with knowledge of how batters adjust their weaknesses, which can be detected by your son just as he stands on the mound. Finally, perhaps your son's greatest obstacle to overcome will be himself. Pitching, besides being a game of intelligence, is perhaps even more so a game of emotions. The trick for your son is to keep these emotions in check and harness all this emotion in a positive way. He should use it to make himself successful and capable of living up to his abilities.

If you and your son can take any of these lessons and put them into practice, you will have justified the writing of this book.

Note: The occasional reference to Jeremy refers to my son who chose to pursue an academic career at Princeton rather than pitch for any one of a number of colleges. During his pitching career, Jeremy utilized most of the techniques described in this book.

CHAPTER 1
PITCHING STRATEGIES - PRELIMINARIES AND PRINCIPLES

Developing a Game Plan

This chapter addresses the issue of developing a pitching strategy for the game. There is no one way to do this, because there are so many different kinds of pitchers, each of whom brings his own strengths and weaknesses to the mound. In addition, how often a pitcher has been seen by the opposing team, as well as what inning he enters the game, the score, and a host of other factors, suggest that no one strategy is the best method to employ at all times. So a variety of strategies will be outlined.

I will provide both pitching principles and pitching tactics, which a pitcher may draw from when developing a game plan. Pitching principles are what might be considered *big picture* ideas. This will include a description of *pitching by the book*, *pitching backwards*, *sequence pitching*, and so on. The section on *tactics* includes a discussion of ideas that may be employed in specific situations or with certain kinds of hitters. This includes how to pitch to pull hitters, when to *climb the ladder,* when not to throw a change-up or curve ball, and so on.

Both pitching principles and tactics are simply tools which your son must become familiar with in order to develop his own pitching game plan.

THE ROLE OF THE PITCHER

In order to develop a strategic approach to pitching, one must first understand the role of the pitcher. This role is commonly misunderstood by many people who watch a baseball game. I've often asked parents while sitting at a youth ball game, "What is the pitcher's goal?" The vast majority of responses were, "To strike out the batter." With so much talk about pitching velocities and strikeout totals, this response is an understandable misconception. But consider a few numbers from the 2005 Major League season.

With 30 teams in the league and every team utilizing a five-man pitching rotation, there were 150 starting pitchers in the 2005 league at the start of the season. Of course this number grew over the course of the season with injuries, demotions, and trades. But working with this baseline number, I ask people, "What percentage of major league starting pitchers averaged just one strikeout per inning in 2005: a) 80%, b) 70% or, c) 55%? Most pick c). Of course they're all wrong because the question is somewhat misleading, and is intended to be just to emphasize my point. In fact, at the end of the 2005 Major League season, only three starting pitchers averaged just one strikeout per inning over the course of the year.

These numbers illustrate the point that the role of a pitcher is not to strike batters out, but instead to just get them out. And the way this is accomplished is by using the other players in the field to catch the fly balls, field the ground balls, and make good throws. A strikeout by a pitcher is simply icing on this cake.

How to Get Outs

The way a pitcher gets these outs is by forcing the batter to hit the ball in ways that he doesn't want to hit it. Quite simply, the pitcher induces the batter to hit off of the end of the bat, over the top of the ball, jammed off of the hands, or contacted just under the ball. Successful hitting is all about timing. The pitcher induces these types of hits by upsetting a batter's timing. This is accomplished by changing the location of the pitches, varying the velocity of the ball, and producing movement on the ball as it heads to the plate. In order to do this, a pitcher uses as his principle tools a repertoire of pitches like the fastball, change-up, curve, sinker, and so forth. All of these pitches, if thrown properly, will upset a batter's timing and prevent solid contact with the ball. And as we will see, sometimes even when a ball is not thrown well, it can still be effective in upsetting the batter's timing on the next pitch.

A pitcher's strategy starts with understanding the batter and what he is trying to do. Understanding the batter requires knowing what he knows, about pitch location and power. Knowing why right-handers bat left, why they open or close their stance, and whether they position themselves forward of the plate or deep in the batter's box, is all based upon an understanding of the strike zone and a player's power contact position.

Understand the Strike Zone

The rules of baseball say that a strike is when any part of the ball passes through any part of the plate, which is 17 inches wide. But it's only when we understand the size of a baseball and think about this statement, that we truly appreciate what this rule implies.

Rule 1 – 09 says that a baseball can be anywhere from 9 to 9 ¼ inches in circumference. Or, approximately 2.86 to 2.94 inches wide. Let's call it 3 inches. When a ball passes over the heart of the plate for a strike, the strike zone is indeed 17 inches. But when the ball nicks the outside corner of the plate with just the outside part of the ball, according to the rules, this too is a strike. Thus any pitch on the corner where only the outside edge of the ball moves through the outside edge of the plate, has now added at least three more inches to that side of the strike zone. An inside pitch on a similar route will add another three inches to the other side of the plate. The strike zone has now increased from 17 to 23 inches wide. Further, in youth ball many umpires will add an additional three inches to the outer corner of the strike zone, raising the total to 26 inches wide. Similarly, in the Major Leagues it is common for pitchers to be given an additional ball width on each side of the plate and not just the outside corner. Most youth ball umpires will also give a similar edge to the pitchers just to keep the game moving and to avoid a game of walks. So your son must realize that the size of the strike zone is considerably larger than the 17 inch plate he's staring in at. It's more like 23 to 26 inches wide. This single fact should help him establish a new and perhaps exciting comfort level.

The Contact Position

Knowing what the strike zone is helps us to understand its size. But it doesn't help us understand where the best place is to make contact with the ball. In fact, in only a few cases the contact point is located inside the actual strike zone itself. Of the inside, middle, and outside pitch, only this last pitch makes contact with the bat, inside the actual strike zone.

For example, in order for the batter to make solid contact with the ball on the inside pitch, the bat must meet the ball about 15 inches in front of the plate. If the hitter waits longer for the ball to travel towards the plate, any contact will produce a foul ball or a pitch jammed off the hands. For a batter to make good contact with a pitch headed for the middle of the plate, he must contact the ball about ten inches in front of the front edge of the plate. And for contact with the outside pitch, the batter can wait until the ball crosses the outside corner of the plate. Although, sometimes even an inch or so beyond this if the batter is trying to *inside-out the* swing to punch a ball down the first base line. But balls hit behind these recommended points of contact produce foul balls, pop ups, or a weakly hit grounder. However, knowing the best contact point for these three pitch locations doesn't tell us where the most power is generated by a batter. And the power location of a batter will help us to understand how to design pitching strategies, so as to avoid it.

A Batter's Power Location

The batter uses a rotational movement in his swing so as to harness the energy generated by this movement. This energy is commonly referred to as torque. The maximum amount of force in a swing is generated by a 90 degree rotation of the hips and upper body. This happens when the hips and torso rotate out of the starting position, with the left shoulder initially pointing at the pitcher, and ending with the chest turned flush to the third baseman. This rotation generates the maximum amount of torque energy, which can then be conveyed through the bat and into the ball. Any rotation of the body which is less than a 90 degree turn will generate less torque, and therefore produce less power.

With this knowledge, it is now clear that the batter can generate the greatest amount of power, when turning into the ***inside*** pitch. A pitch on the outside corner requires only a 30 to 35 degree body rotation and thus generates less torque, and therefore less force is applied to the ball. When contact is made with a middle of the strike zone pitch, out in front of the plate, somewhat more torque is generated than on an outside pitch; but it is still less than a full 90 degree rotation, which is generated on the inside pitch.

We now understand where the maximum power location is for all batters. It's on the inside pitch. However, this does not mean that a batter can't hit a ball over the fence on an outside pitch. Power hitters are dangerous in all fields and must be pitched accordingly. But knowing where all batters will generate their most powerful swings is a key piece of information to know when developing a pitching strategy.

How Pitches Move

Knowing how each pitch moves as it nears the plate is key to designing a pitching strategy. It explains why natural right-handers switch over and swing from the left side of the plate. It also explains why left-handed pitchers are brought in to pitch to left-handed power hitters. And why these match-ups are usually in the pitcher's favor.

Fastball – The four-seam fastball often moves in a straight line to the plate. But if it has any movement, it is towards the glove side.

Cutter – Like the four-seamer, but more dramatically, this fastball moves towards the glove side.

The Sinker – Another kind of fastball, it is held with a two-seam grip but as a consequence of its one o'clock release point, moves the opposite way. It moves toward the throwing-hand side.

The Forkball – By wedging the ball between the first two fingers and deep into the hand, the pitcher will generate a slower moving ball, with a deep drop at the end of the pitch.

The Split Finger – This is a hybrid pitch, somewhere between a fastball and a forkball. With a narrower split of the fingers and less of a choking grip than with the forkball, the wrist can generate more of a snap. The pitch moves to the glove side and down.

The Curve – A 12 – 6 curve breaks downward more than the 11 – 5 ball. But both still move towards the glove side.

The Slider – Like the splitter, the slider is a combination of two pitches. It combines the velocity of a fastball with the break of a curve. It moves towards the glove side with a late break down.

The Circle Change-Up – The *window shade* release of this pitch usually causes the ball to break slightly to the glove side. An *over-the-top* release will create an even bigger break to the throwing hand side.

The Palm Ball – Early practitioners of this pitch, like Walter Johnson, held the ball deep in the palm secured by only the thumb and little finger on the side of the ball. The other three fingers are just along for the ride. A snap of the wrist at release, results in a slow moving pitch breaking slightly to the glove side.

The Screwball – The release of this pitch, with a rotation of the hand in the opposite direction of the wrist-turn for a slider or curve, results in the ball breaking down and towards the throwing-hand side. The hand actually turns outward so that it finishes with the palm opened up toward the third base line. Christy Mathewson, who is credited with inventing the screwgie, called it his *fade-away pitch*. He sued this pitch so regularly that when he finally retired his walking gate down the street would be with the palm of his pitching hand turned outwards, rather than inwards like everyone else.

The Knuckler – The intent of this pitch is for the ball to release out of the hand with as little rotation as possible. The varying directions of the wind will cause the ball to sink, swerve, or jump in all directions. Only the weatherman may know where this pitch will end up.

PITCH LOCATION TABLE

THE PITCH	**IT'S MOVEMENT**
Fastball	Straight/glove side
Cutter	Glove side
Sinker	Throwing hand side and down
Forkball	Down with slight movement to glove side
Split Finger	To glove side
Curveball	To glove side and down
Slider	To glove side and down
Circle Change-up	To glove side and down
Palm Ball	To glove side and down
Screwball	To hand side
Knuckleball	Anyone's guess

The Left-Handed Hitter and Lefty-Lefty Match-Ups

It's now clear why a natural right-handed player learns to hit from the left side. These players understand that the majority of pitchers that they will face are right-handed. They also know that, as indicated in the above table, the majority of balls out of the pitcher's hand will be moving towards the pitcher's glove side and to the left side of the plate. That is, right into the left-hander's power zone inside. That's why natural righties learn to hit from the left side.

Similar reasoning applies when the coach brings in a southpaw to pitch to a left-handed batter. The strength of this match-up for the pitcher is in the fact that most of his pitches will be moving to the right side of the plate, away from the lefty's power zone. Hitting moving pitches away from the left-handed batter often results in weakly-hit grounders or fly balls, which is exactly what this lefty-lefty match-up is intended to do.

Back up and Back Door Pitches

The notes above describe how a pitch moves when thrown towards its natural location. That is, a cutter thrown to the outside of the plate has a natural motion to that same side. At times, with certain pitches like the curve, this break can be quite large. But what happens when such a pitch is thrown to the opposite side of the plate? That is, what happens when a cut fastball is thrown to the inside of the plate?

Throwing pitches to the opposite side of the plate, away from the direction of their natural motion, won't change the fundamental movement of the ball. But it will lessen the degree to which such a pitch will break.

For example, if a curveball breaks 12 to 15 inches when thrown to the pitcher's glove side, this break may be only four to six inches when thrown to the pitcher's hand-side of the plate. Usually such a pitch is initially thrown *off* of the plate. But then, with a reduced break, it drifts back over the corner. When this pitch is thrown to a right-handed batter, it is called a *back-up* pitch. This is because a hitter will often back away from the plate, thinking that he's going to be hit by the ball. But then it breaks back over the plate for a strike. Such a pitch, when thrown to the same location but with a left hander at bat, also starts off of the plate, but again drifts back over the southpaw's outside corner, as a *backdoor* strike. It will be important for your son to try throwing all of his pitches to both sides of the plate, just to see how they react. He may discover that he has a natural *back-up* or *backdoor* pitch in his repertoire.

Where to Stand on the Rubber

The rules require that the pitcher begin his delivery with at least one foot in contact with the rubber. The foot may be on top of the pitcher's plate or just beside it, so long as the foot is in some contact with it. However, on which side of the rubber should your son stand?

There is no definitive answer to this question. It will be determined by which pitches your son throws and how these pitches move.

For example, if your son throws a fastball which has just a little break towards his glove side, then by standing on the right side of the rubber as he faces the plate actually can help him. Firstly, most of the batters he will see are right-handed. Plus, he will want to throw most of his fastballs away from this batter. So by standing to the right side of the pitcher's plate, the ball will be moving across the plate, which is the same direction of the *natural movement* of most fastballs: from hand side towards glove side. Because he's throwing towards the direction of the pitch's natural movement, this will even help to add a little more break to this pitch.

On the other hand, if your son were to stand on the left side of the rubber facing home, he would be throwing *against the grain* of the pitch's natural movement. If his fastball has only a little break to it, throwing against the grain will straighten the pitch right out. Added break always makes a pitch harder to hit, whereas a pitch moving on a straight line is a lot easier to hit. So, if he stands on the left side of the rubber, his fastball will straighten out and it thus becomes much easier to hit.

What If He Has Three Pitches?

Knowing in which direction a pitch will naturally break is the starting point for deciding where to stand. If your son throws a *fastball* with a little movement away from the right-hander, a *sinker* that breaks *in* on the righty, and a *change-up* that stays on a straight line, then the reasoning is simple. He probably spots his fastball the best and will also use it the most. So throw from the right side, because his fastball will benefit greatly and thus be more effective than his sinker. In these circumstances, cater to the fastball. Besides, the change-up won't be affected by where he stands.

However, the decision becomes more difficult when he throws a very effective sinker and change-up, and both pitches break in on the right-hander. By moving over to the left side, these pitches will develop even more of that inside break, because he will be throwing *with the grain*. But not only can they be very effective against the right-hander inside, but outside as well. Both of these pitches can be thrown outside, off of the plate against the righty who, seeing them outside will give up on them. But then because of their normal movement, they break back and cross the outside corner of the plate, as *backdoor pitches*. Pitches like this literally paralyze batters. So now when your son throws his fastball away but off of the plate, unlike his sinker the fastball won't move back over the plate. Instead, the pitch stays outside, off the plate. But the batter, worrying that this is your son's other fastball (sinker) and knowing it can *backdoor* the plate, will now get caught swinging at pitches that he shouldn't.

In addition, both the sinker and change-up can be very effective pitches against the left-handed batter. Both of these pitches normally will be breaking away from this hitter, usually resulting in weakly hit balls, when any contact is made at all. These are often easy outs. Although some breaking movements on his fastball will indeed be sacrificed from pitching from this side of the rubber, in these circumstances the cost will be greatly outweighed by other advantages. A pitcher with these kinds of pitches should set up on the left side of the pitcher's plate. You and your son should discuss where he should stand based upon what pitches he throws, and how each pitch will break. Now determine how to maximize his effectiveness.

Let him practice from each side and see what works best for him. But one approach should be avoided: don't let him move from one side to the other side of the rubber, depending upon which pitch he intends to throw. If he does this, it won't be long before the other team figures out that pitching from one side means sinkers and from the other side, it's the curve or fastball that's coming.

Contact Zone, Advantages and Disadvantages

Knowing where and how a batter tries to make contact with the ball suggests certain advantages and disadvantages for each area. For example, although the *inside* pitch offers the advantage of maximum power, because contact has to be made so far out in front of the plate, it brings with it a real disadvantage. The hitter must get his bat moving very early if he hopes to catch up to a hard pitch on the inside corner. If a player does not have a quick reaction time, this may be an unhittable pitch.

On the other hand, a batter can wait longer for a pitch on the *outside* corner., but this location does not offer the same kind of power advantages as an inside pitch. In addition, since most balls are moving away from the batter, these hits frequently result in weakly contacted balls, often for easy outs.

One would think that making contact with the *middle* of the plate pitch would maximize advantages while minimizing the disadvantages of other pitches. This is true, insofar as this thinking goes. It is true that a hitter can wait a little longer for the middle pitch to arrive than with the inside pitch, plus generate more power than he will be able to on the outside pitch. But there's a problem: most pitchers are trying to keep the ball away from the middle part of the plate, specifically because it is the killing ground for so many batters. At least that should be the strategy of any parent of a pitcher reading this book.

The Value of Pitching Strategies

This chapter will outline pitching ***principles*** as well as introducing ***tactics*** which a pitcher may wish to employ during a game. All of the ideas explained in this chapter are employed throughout baseball by both coaches and pitchers alike. But it is worth noting that these ideas are not always consistent with one another. For example, as you will see, the theory of pitching *by the book* is in direct conflict with the theory of pitching *backwards*. Nonetheless, both approaches can work depending upon the pitcher and the circumstances of the game. Similarly, the generally accepted tactic of not throwing a change-up in a 0 – 2 count should be ignored if the pitcher has great command of this pitch.

The value of your son being introduced to a variety of pitching strategies has three very real advantages. First, it provides him with the baseline knowledge which pitchers need to know when developing their own approach to the game. Second, by developing a pitching strategy for a game, your son has something specific from which to adapt when he starts to be hit by a batter or a team. If he does not have a strategy for the game, when he is hit, he has nothing to adjust because he hasn't been pitching in any specific fashion. Anything he adjusts will just be based on guesswork. This is never a preferred approach.

Finally and perhaps most importantly, when developing a game strategy, your son will be required to *think* about what he intends to do. It will compel him to understand how the game is played and then develop a game plan based upon this knowledge. Not enough young players begin thinking about the game early enough. This chapter is intended to give him plenty of ideas about what hitters and pitchers are trying to do.

PITCHING PRINCIPLES
Keep It Simple

Although this chapter will provide many views on principles and strategies for pitching, your son must always remember one rule: *Keep it simple*! In building pitching mechanics, he should choose two or three ideas, master their application, and then add more. Your son will only become confused if he tries to implement all of these pitching ideas at once. This confusion will breed uncertainty, which will only prevent him from throwing a quality pitch. He should start with the ones he can implement now and as his abilities grow, gradually absorb more ideas into his repertoire. But even then, thinking too much can still get the best of pitchers into trouble. Over time and with experience, he will develop an instinct for his game. *Instinctive pitching* is the most effective approach.

Always Throw Strikes

No one is going to be intimidated by a pitcher who can't hit the strike zone, no matter how hard he throws. Even free swingers will realize that all they have to do in order to get to first base is wait. So your son must throw strikes in order to be taken seriously.

Many young pitchers are afraid to be hit and so they often pick at corners, for fear of solid contact. More often than not, they miss their target. Their problem is that they've forgotten the role of the pitcher and the purpose of their defense. It's the defense that gets the batter out on fly balls and grounders. But if pitches aren't over the plate, then no one will be swinging the bat, and there won't be any fly balls or grounders with which a defender can make a play.

In addition, all pitching strategies like working *hard to soft* or throwing by *the book*, are premised upon a pitcher being able to throw strikes. If your son can't, or won't, throw into the zone, then he won't be able to implement any strategy for success.

Don't Always Throw Strikes

Being known as a pitcher who throws strikes has the advantage that hitters start swinging at pitches that aren't in the strike zone. A few years ago Sports Weekly published a comparison between two starting pitchers, each from the Atlanta Braves and the Arizona Diamondbacks. This article compared the pitching performances of the "old guard" Greg Maddux and Tom Glavine of the Braves, and the "new guard" Randy Johnson and Curt Schilling from Arizona. All of these pitchers had a reputation as great pitchers who throw strikes. But this article illustrated a curious statistic. When tracking the pitches of all of these all-star pitchers, it was discovered that they all threw in the strike zone only 47 or 48 percent of the time. More than half of their pitches were not over the plate!

What does this mean? Does this suggest that these great pitchers are not as accurate as we all imagined? Absolutely not. These statistics reflect a couple of things. First, at the major league level, with batters as good as they are, pitchers simply cannot throw in the strike zone all of the time, without being hit hard. However, these pitchers have proven that they can throw strikes so consistently that the batter swings at some pitches outside of the strike zone. Just because he isn't sure whether the ball is, or is not, over the plate.

By having established their ability to throw strikes when they want to, these pitchers can now throw pitches which are intended to miss the plate. Greg Maddux characterizes one of his "commandments of pitching" this way: "Make the balls look like strikes, and the strikes look like balls." This has always been one of his secrets for pitching success.

There are a couple of other lessons to be learned from this. Young pitchers must start out throwing strikes in order to put the ball in play and get outs. Soon they will become known for their ability to put the ball over the plate, which in turn will create apprehension in the batter. An apprehensive hitter is always a good thing. Second, when your son reaches senior levels of play, this reputation will help him get strikes even when he throws pitches just inside or outside the plate. A high ball or low pitch out of the zone become easy outs or missed pitches, all because your son is known for his ability to throw strikes. Putting this philosophy into play and gaining the ability to get these easy outs is dependent upon one thing: knowing how to throw strikes.

Two to One Ratio

Throw twice as many strikes as balls. This is the statistical goal that your son should be aiming for in every game. It is a statistical barometer for telling him whether he has command of his pitches. Anything better than a two to one ratio is great!

Command the Fastball

Leo Mazzone writes, "Everything works off the command, not the velocity, of the fastball" High-end velocity is great, but not if you can't hit your spots. Even a slower-moving fastball will be more effective that the top-end heater, because it can be used to set up the batter. It will have the hitter looking for pitches in one area, while your son is throwing it somewhere else. And the better a pitcher's command, the more choices of strategies he has to implement.

First-Pitch Strikes

The most successful pitchers throw their first pitch for a strike. A first-pitch strike lowers the hitting success of major leaguers by 100 points. By the pitcher getting ahead with a strike, the batter becomes more apprehensive. Batters worry more about a pitch on either corner being called for another strike. This causes the hitter to swing at pitches that are out of the strike zone. In effect, by getting ahead of the batter, the pitcher has widened the strike zone. Batters become ***jumpier*** and thus tend to swing too early. This usually results in popups or ground-ball outs. In addition, by getting ahead of the batter with a first-pitch strike, a pitcher now has the option to use any strategy he wants in going after the hitter.

Pitching by the Book

Pitching by the book refers to generally accepted ideas about the generic type of pitch to throw with certain pitch counts. For example, in a 0-0 count, the pitcher must try to throw a first-pitch strike and get ahead of the batter. With every strike a batter's average can fall by as much as 100 points. Thus in this instance, the pitcher should throw his best pitch, which is usually a fastball.

In a 0-1 count, since the pitcher has already gotten ahead of the batter with a fastball, an off-speed pitch could fool him for another strike. So the pitcher now has a choice of pitches to throw.

In a 0-2 count, the pitcher is way ahead of the batter. A purpose pitch is usually recommended. This could be a fastball high out of the strike zone. This would move the batter's eyes and set him up for a low pitch, inside or outside. Or, a slow moving breaking pitch (i.e. curve), also out of the strike zone, would show the hitter a slow moving target. Coming back on the next pitch with a low fastball will make it difficult for the batter to adjust his timing to catch up to the heat. But in both cases, with the pitcher so far ahead, this pitch must not be a hittable one or else a great opportunity could be wasted. So in this instance, even a bouncing breaking ball can be useful.

In a 1-0 count, the pitcher must throw a strike. So he should go to his most reliable pitch, the fastball.

In a 1-1 count, get ahead. So go back to the reliable fastball.

In a 1-2 count, the pitcher is ahead and so he can play a little bit. An off-speed ball can induce the easy out for a called strike.

In a 2-0 count, the pitcher is behind, so he must throw his reliable fastball for a strike.

In a 2-1 count, the pitcher is still behind, so he should throw his fastball to catch-up.

In a 2-2 count, the pitcher is actually ahead, even though the count is even. Since the batter has seen so many fastballs, off-speed pitches are effective for an out.

In a 3-0 count, the pitcher is so far behind he must throw a fastball for a strike.

In a 3-1 count, the pitcher is still behind and a strike is needed. Throw a fastball.

In a 3-2 count, the pitcher must still avoid walking the batter. Again go back to the reliable fastball for the out.

But these recommendations are not set in stone. On some days, a pitcher won't be able to hit the back stop with his fastball, so whenever a strike is needed (i.e. 3-0) he must go to whatever pitch is working best for him that day. However, for the most part, these are widely accepted recommendations when a pitcher has pretty good control of his pitches.

TABLE 1: PITCHING BY THE BOOK

Count	Pitch	Pitcher
0-0	Fastball	Even
0-1	Off speed/Fastball	Ahead
0-2	Breaking/High Fastball	Ahead
1-0	Fastball	Behind
1-1	Off speed/Fastball	Even
1-2	Off speed	Ahead
2-0	Fastball	Behind
2-1	Fastball	Behind
2-2	Off speed/fastball	Even
3-0	Fastball	Behind
3-1	Fastball	Behind
3-2	Fastball	Even

Pitching Backwards

This heading would be more aptly called *pitching against the Book,* or *pitching opposite of the Book.* This is because pitching backwards recommends that in those counts in which *the Book* calls for a fastball, you should throw an off-speed pitch. And in off-speed counts, throw the heater.

Remember, the goal of the pitcher is to upset the batter's timing. Since batters too will familiarize themselves with *the Book's* recommendations for pitch counts, a pitcher will upset the batter's timing by throwing a pitch that the hitter doesn't expect. Since the hitter knows *the Book* calls for a certain pitch in this count, then throw the opposite pitch. The strategy of pitching backwards is simply a throwing the unexpected pitch.

TABLE 2: PITCHING BACKWARDS

Count	Pitch
0-0	Off speed
0-1	Fastball/Breaking - choice
0-2	Fastball
1-0	Off speed
1-1	Off speed
1-2	Fastball
2-0	Off speed
2-1	Fastball/ Off speed
2-2	Fastball/ Off speed - choice
3-0	Off speed
3-1	Off speed
3-2	Off speed

Use Both Approaches

Neither *pitching by the book* nor *pitching backwards* will always work if your son only uses one of these systems. This is because pitching with just one approach will soon be detected and a pitcher then becomes predictable. Whenever this occurs, balls soon start leaving the ballpark. So pitchers must mix these two approaches together on different days and in varying degrees. Or, use one approach the first time through the order and then switch to the other strategy the next time he sees the batter. Then adjust again, on the third go around with the hitter. Your son must simply mix up the approaches in such a way so that he does not become predictable.

Dominant Hand Theory

Dominant hand theory is not so much a specific pitch count strategy as it may be a way for your son to decide what to throw when he is uncertain about the strengths and weakness of the batter.

Dominant hand theory is premised upon the idea that we all have physical characteristics that have evolved because one side of our body plays a more dominant role in our lives. For example, a right-handed person usually has a stronger right hand and arm than the left. Similarly, the right-handed person's stronger right leg will cause him to take a longer stride with the right leg than with his left. As a consequence of these physical tendencies, both right-handed and left-handed batters also have natural strengths and weaknesses. Pitchers can use this knowledge to their advantage.

Statistics have shown that right-handed hitters often have trouble hitting the ball in two specific areas, while they usually are better at making contact in two other areas. Right-handed batters are good at hitting the low-and-away pitch, and the up-and-in pitch. On the other hand, they have trouble with the high-and-away ball, as well as the low-and-inside pitch. Left-handers, on the other hand, are strong low and inside, as well as up and away, the very opposite strength location of righties. The lefty, though, has more trouble with the up-and-in ball, as well as the low-and-away pitch.

When looking at a diagram of a lefty and a righty batter standing at the plate together, it becomes obvious that the areas of strengths and weakness for both batters are coincidentally in the exact same places in relation to the plate (see Figure #1). The right hander's strength on down and away is in the same strong low-and-inside location for the left hander. Similarly, the lefty's weak area of high and inside is the same weak area for the righty, except that the right hander calls this location high and away. This coincidence of strength and weakness locations, should help your son remember where to pitch when he faces an unknown batter, a free swinger, or is simply unsure of where to throw his next pitch. But if he has trouble remembering each of the batter's hot and cold spots, here's a useful hint.

All your son should remember is one hot spot for either the left-hander or right-handed batter. For example, a hot spot for a lefty is low and inside. With this information, now all your son must remember is to find the other hot spot with a diagonal line. Thus using a diagonal line, your son can remember that the lefty's other hot spot is high and away. Therefore, the lefty's cold spots are the other two locations that are left not connected by the diagonal line: high and inside, and low and away. Remembering that the right-hander's hot and cold spots are in the same physical areas as the left-hander, your son can now figure out the righty's hot and cold spots. All he has to do is remember one hot spot for a lefty or righty, and then match it up using a diagonal line.

Pitching Hard to Soft

This strategy for a pitcher builds upon the belief that a hard thrown pitch, such as a fastball or cutter, is a good way to set up a batter for a softer pitch, like the curve. The faster pitch generates a certain apprehension in the batter. He knows that he's going to have to be quick in his reaction times if he wants to make solid contact with the ball. So he's inclined to start his swing early or jump at the next pitch in order to make sure that he gets there on time. But because he's so aggressive, he's now vulnerable to a slower moving pitch. By the time he recognizes that the pitch is not a fastball, he's already committed to it and it's very difficult to pull the body back off of the pitch. Often his hands roll over in the swing because he swung too early. Any contact will now result in a weakly hit fly ball or grounder. Alternatively, if he does pull off of the ball, a breaking pitch over the plate can buckle his knees and will be called as a strike.

Working *hard to soft* works because the pitcher is feeding off of the batter's apprehension about the fastball, and the hitter's inability to sit patiently and wait on the pitch. This approach requires using about 75 to 80 percent hard pitches (i.e. fastball, cutters, etc.) and 20 to 25 percent soft, like a change-up or curve. The hard pitch must be thrown a high percentage of the time in order to put into the mind of the batter that the next pitch will also be a fastball. If the pitcher throws an even number of hard and soft pitches, the batter won't be anticipating a fastball, so he'll sit back and wait longer. The pitcher's advantage will then be lost.

Pitching Soft to Hard

Some pitchers prefer to pitch *soft to hard.* Perhaps the best known of these is Boston's Tim Wakefield. Wakefield is one of the few knuckleball pitchers around and he throws it a lot. He'll also mix in a curveball with it. By his establishing the probability of a soft pitch coming next, Wakefield then throws his fastball. His fastball is only in the high seventy to eighty miles per hour range and should never get past a major league hitter. But it does. The fastball is effective specifically because he throws so many curves and knuckleballs. So the hitter's *sit soft* and Wakefield throws his fastball past a batter, because he's not expecting it.

Like pitching *hard to soft,* working the fastball off of change-ups, curves and knuckleballs only works because the batter is not expecting it. But working *soft to hard* is more difficult than the traditional approach, because the pitcher has to throw a lot of slow stuff. Usually 50 percent or so of the pitches are off speed of one variety or another. But inevitably, batters are going to guess right sometimes and then the pitcher could be hit hard. It takes both great control and a sizeable helping of courage, for a pitcher to use the *soft to hard* strategy on a regular basis.

Never Give in to the Plate

One of Leo Mazzone's cardinal rules is that the pitcher must never give in to the plate. What he means by this is that the pitcher must never throw the ball over the middle of the plate.

Tom Glavine, John Smoltz and Greg Maddux have all had success pitching using this simple philosophy of throwing only over the outer thirds of the plate. These are usually the less dangerous areas for the pitchers.

Mazzone emphasizes:

> "The strategy is 'don't give in to the strike zone.' It's the one thing you must remember if you want to be a successful pitcher. It's not a matter of giving in to the hitter. The mentality is to not even care about the hitter per se – it's the strike zone you want to focus on."

Pitch Halves to Thirds

Leo Mazzone teaches his pitchers to throw to the inside and outside thirds of the plate. The middle third is right over the center of the plate and should always be avoided. This is the area which Maddux and other Mazzone disciples are referring to when they advise, "Never give in to the strike zone." Whether one is throwing something hard or soft, he must stay on the edges of the plate and avoid its middle.

This is sound philosophy for higher levels of pitching. It also helps us to understand how a ball continually thrown over the outer third of the plate can be made to look like a strike when it is thrown just off of the corner. Being able to consistently pitch to the inner and outer thirds is the stepping stone to making balls look like strikes, and strikes look like balls.

But at lower levels, breaking the plate down into thirds is too much to ask of a young player. Your son should begin by just throwing at the plate within the high-low strike zone boundaries. As he improves his accuracy, he can then divide the plate into two halves. All of the tactics and strategies outlined in this book can be implemented with the use of this breakdown. This two-part division will also help your son to develop his focus but not require him to hit unreasonable goals, like painting the corners of the plate. After he improves his control, divide the plate into thirds, and see what he can do.

The Necessity of Pitching Inside

Pitchers learn very early in their careers that a batter's power numbers are built upon hitting the inside pitch. For this reason, many pitchers at all levels are reluctant to throw inside. But this is a critical mistake. In order for a pitcher to be effective, he must control the strike zone. This includes the inner part of it.

Most pitchers are taught to throw pitches which are either on the outside corner or are at least moving in that direction (i.e. curves, slider). Any contact with these pitches is less likely to be solid and therefore are balls hit for catchable outs. But batters know this so they are taught to crowd the plate and extend their arms to make better contact. Thus no pitcher will have success on the pitches away, if he allows the hitter to reach to the outside corner.

Your son's response to this problem is to demonstrate to the hitter that he will come inside with his pitches. A number of points are worth remembering. First, your son doesn't have to live in there. He need only keep the batter honest by demonstrating that he is prepared to throw strikes inside. Second, although this may be where the hitter generates his greatest power, he still has to catch up to this pitch. Remember where the batter must make contact with the ball. Usually it's a foot and a-half or so out in front of the hitter's front foot. This takes very quick hands for a hitter to be able to react to a fastball inside. Because of the lesser amount of time that the batter will have to react to this pitch, it will seem like your son has added two or three more miles per hour to this pitch. Third, by throwing the pitch inside, your son is less predictable. This should help slow down the batter's reaction time for all pitches. And lastly, when he goes inside, ensure that he keeps the ball down. Throw beneath the thighs for strikes. If he wants to move a batter back off of the plate, brush him back with a ball off of the inside corner and just below the hands. It's surprising how many batters offer at this kind of pitch which is out of the strike zone. But one way or another, it will keep the hitter from crowding the plate and give back to your son, the outside corner.

Throwing Inside Provides a Tactic

If your son throws inside regularly, the batter must adjust and be ready for this pitch. Plus when your son throws inside, he will usually throw something hard (fastball, cutter, etc.) because he knows the batter will have to start early in order to make solid contact out in front of the plate. This is not easy to do, so the hitter will have to adjust in order to catch up to the pitch. But when he does this, most young batters begin *jumping* at the pitch. He's too aggressive, which now makes him vulnerable for a slower breaking ball on the outside corner, a pitch that the batter normally has to wait on in order to make solid contact. By throwing inside regularly, your son now has a new tactic to use. It is commonly referred to as *hard in, soft away.*

Only Pitch Inside When Ahead in the Count

Coaches like Leo Mazzone believe that a pitcher should pitch inside only when he is ahead in the count. They understand that pitching inside is necessary to keep a batter from crowding the plate and taking away the outside pitch. But they also realize that pitching inside is where the hitter can generate his greatest power. So these pitches have to be made judiciously. First get ahead in the count by throwing low and away. A pitcher should try to get to 0-1, 0-2, or 1-2 by staying away and using off-speed pitches. Then, when the batter is looking for the next pitch on the outside, come inside hard on the corner for a strike. But keep the ball off the heart of the plate. Even if your son misses the inside corner he won't be hurt and he still has a favorable count. Meanwhile, he's kept the batter from crowding the plate because the hitter is now aware that if he does, he'll have no chance on a pitch over the inside corner.

Pitch to Your Strengths

The pitching strategies and tactics outlined in this chapter and the next are just tools for your son to use when developing a game plan or if he is uncertain what pitch to throw. But when he is in trouble or a tight situation (i.e. 3-2 count), there is a guiding principle to follow: throw your best pitch. Even if the batter's best skill is in hitting the best pitch you throw, he still has to hit it solidly. And he doesn't know where you're going to throw it. Your son still has the advantages.

Every pitcher should pitch to his own strengths. Even if his strength is also the batter's strength. If your son has a good fastball and he needs a strike, then throw it. Even if it means throwing it to a fastball hitter. If your son needs a strike but is afraid to throw his fastball to a fastball hitter, then he's throwing his second or even third best pitch. He's now allowing the other team to determine what he throws. In fact, he's letting the opposition determine his pitching strategy. This is a recipe for disaster.

So encourage your son to always be aggressive and go after the batter. Make the hitter beat your son on his best pitch.

Remember, even if the batter knows what's coming, he still has to execute properly in order to hit the ball.

Know Your Pitches Today

No pitcher, at any level, throws his pitches with the same accuracy and movement every game. On some days the curve will be biting, while on other days it's just going to hang over the plate. Your son must determine as early as possible which pitch he commands well today. He should also figure out which pitch he can't command, but which he can nevertheless throw over the plate, somewhere. Then build or adjust his strategy accordingly.

But remind him that just because a pitch may not be working in his warm-up, this doesn't mean he won't find it later in the game. In counts where he is ahead, he may wish to try the pitch again. Many pitchers find that a pitch which didn't work early in the game comes alive two or three innings later. Again, this is another advantage of getting ahead of the batters with early strikes. It gives the pitcher the luxury of going back to a pitch to try it out again.

Throw Quality Pitches

Your son will better appreciate the value of his pitching if he can understand that his principle goal is to always throw a quality pitch. A *quality pitch* is not just a third-pitch strike. In fact, it doesn't have to actually even be a strike at all. A quality pitch can best be described as any pitch which simply *serves a purpose*. This may indeed be a third pitch strike for the out but a quality pitch can also be a *purpose ball* in the dirt. A hard curveball that fools the batter into almost swinging can be a quality pitch even if it bounces across the plate for a strike. This is because it can set up the batter for the next pitch, a hard thrown pitch over the inside corner of the plate for the out.

Even when a pitch is hit, if your son has off-set the batter's timing resulting in him making poor contact for a pop fly or easy out, this too can be a quality pitch. But, throwing quality pitches requires that your son stays alert and always keep his head in the game. Only in this way can he take advantage of *quality pitches* to get the out.

Location and Movement Trump Velocity

Greg Maddux's second commandment of pitching is: "Movement and location trump velocity, every time." None of the pitching strategies or tactics outlined in this book will work unless a player can hit his desired location. A strike-throwing pitcher who throws soft is still feared more than any flame thrower who can't hit the strike zone. And pitchers who constantly leave the ball thigh-high over the middle of the plate never last very long at any level of play.

Location pitchers become even more successful when they can add movement to their pitches. With movement, a strike-throwing pitcher can induce the batter to swing at pitches that move towards the strike zone, but tail away just as they reach it. A curveball thrown out of the zone can break in the ***back door*** at the last minute for a called strike. These are Maddux's "balls that look like strikes," and "strikes which start out looking like balls," out of the strike zone. A pitcher's success is only enhanced when he can add movement to his pitches. Coach "Spanky" McFarland will remind all young pitchers that, "One inch of movement is worth two miles per hour." Looking at this another way, if your son's pitches have lots of movement, then he doesn't ***need*** to throw hard to still be effective.

All Kinds of Velocity

Velocity is a great pitching tool, but it is most effective when the pitcher understands how to use it. As mentioned earlier, flame throwers can be effective because batters at all levels can be intimidated by high-end velocity. But batters at all levels can also time this high-end heat and when they do, the ball goes for a ride.

So, ensure that your son isn't throwing hard all of the time. Change-ups and curves can upset a hitter's timing, but so can a fastball thrown with just a little less velocity than the last one your son threw, as can a ball thrown just a little harder than the last fastball thrown. The ability to vary the speed of the fastball only makes this pitch more effective.

The Better the Command, the More Complex the Game Plan

For young, inexperienced pitchers, many of the ideas in this chapter will be new. They will have to be consciously adopted into their game plan. For example, throwing first-pitch strikes and throwing the first pitch away from the batter will initially have to be focused on by your son. But as his command improves, he will find that these goals are soon second nature to him and he won't need to focus on them so specifically. Then, as his command of the strike zone improves, he will be able to adopt these and other approaches and absorb them as second nature as well. Although your son must always try to keep things simple, greater command of his pitches will permit him a broader choice of strategies to implement. All the while, still choosing just a few to use as he keeps everything simple and within his capabilities.

Understand a Batter's Vision

Pitchers must remember that we all see an object moving towards us better than we see one moving away. This has obvious implications for a pitcher throwing a breaking ball. For example, if a right-handed pitcher throws a curve ball to a left-handed hitter, the batter will have an easier time tracking the movement of this pitch as it breaks towards him, than if it was moving away from him. This fact about a person's *active visual acuity* helps us to understand why managers try to match up left-handed pitchers with left-handed batters. Besides the fact that the righty's pitches are all moving in towards a lefty's power zone, the pitches themselves are actually easier for the batter to see than if he was facing those of a southpaw, whereas the lefthanders curve ball or slider would be moving away from the hitter.

Although most pitches from a right-handed pitcher will be moving in towards the left-handed batter and are therefore easier for him to pick up, a pitcher is particularly vulnerable on big breaking pitches. The reason for this is simple. Pitches like the cutter and split finger fastball are moving much faster than a pitch like the curve ball. On a curve, the batter has more time to adjust to the slower break. Although your son must be willing to throw all of his pitches to both lefties and righties, he should always be aware of how one's active visual acuity makes some pitches more dangerous to throw to some batters than to others.

Off-Speed Pitches Work

Your son should watch what most batters are trying to do in batting cages or in batting practice before a game. Almost none of them are trying to take the ball the other way or drive the ball past the pitcher. Just about every batter is trying to pull the ball hard. In order to do this, they have to start their hands early and commit the body.

So use this knowledge. It explains why batters are vulnerable to any off-speed pitch, whether it breaks or not. It's because the batter is trying to get out early, with a better jump on the fastball. But a slower moving off-speed pitch will cause most batters to commit too soon. Consequently they turn their wrists over prematurely, resulting most often in a weakly hit ground ball. So encourage your son to throw off-speed pitches because off-speed pitches work.

Pitching Sequences

Pitching sequences refers to the practice of a pitcher determining, before the game, what pitches he will throw and in what order. In many older youth ball leagues, a pitcher will develop pitching sequences dependent upon his knowledge of other teams. At younger levels of play, where the particular tendencies of a batter are unknown, *sequencing* can still be an effective tool.

For example, if your son throws a fastball, change-up, sinker, and curveball, he may decide to use the following pitch sequence for a right-handed batter.

1. Fastball – low and away
2. Fastball – low and away
3. Curveball – low and away
4. Sinker – low and inside
5. Fastball – low and away
6. Change up – low and inside

This sequence works ***hard to soft***. The majority of the pitches are a form of fastball. It works hard outside, a change of speed, and a break, still low and away, and then to the opposite side of the plate. Then there is a change of pace. In this way, location movement, and velocity variations are used to throw this batter's timing off.

The second right-handed batter will see:

1. Fastball – low and away
2. Sinker – low and inside
3. Fastball – high and inside (at hands)
4. Change up – low and away
5. Curve – low and away
6. Sinker – low and inside

This sequence once again includes changes in velocity, location, and movement.

These two sequences will be alternated with each right-handed hitter. For a lefty, he would see:

1. Sinker – low and away
2. Sinker – low and away
3. Fastball – high and inside (at hands)
4. Change up – low and away
5. Sinker – low and away
6. Curve – backdoor, low and away

Again: location, movement, and velocity are varied in order to keep the batter off balance. Because there are so few left-handed hitters, only one sequence may be all that your son needs for this game.

Sequence pitching is a useful tool because it eliminates uncertainty. Pitchers go into the game with more confidence if they have a prepared plan of attack. It eliminates tentative pitching, which a player often does when he only decides what he's going to do pitch-to-pitch. It also provides a player with an easier ability to adjust later in the game, when the opposition starts to figure out the pitching patterns. Additionally, once again a pitcher's overall appreciation for how this game can be played improves tremendously when he is required to think about his pitching patterns.

Sequencing Imposes Demands

Pitching sequences make certain demands upon pitchers, which should be understood before sequencing is used. Most importantly, it requires that a pitcher understand his strengths and weaknesses. It's not very useful to set up a sequence of pitches that the player can't execute. Sequencing also places a premium on command. If your son can't yet throw with some accuracy to the sides of the plate, then sequencing is less valuable. Although, even without a strong command of his pitches, it is still useful since he will be changing velocities and inducing movement on the ball. A player should also be prepared to move to another set of pitches when he realizes that his opposition has figured out his throwing pattern. This can sometimes happen the second time through the lineup, provided the hitter thinks about what has happened to him previously. But your son should not alter his sequence pattern too early. Make them prove that they've figured it out by actually hitting the ball. Don't adjust before there is a need to.

Additionally, sequence pitching requires that the pitcher and catcher be on the same page. Your son must tell the catcher what sequences he intends to use before they take to the field. If your son is constantly having to shake off the catcher's calls, his pitching rhythm will be interrupted and his frustration level will probably climb. This is only to the hitter's advantage. Besides, the catcher may have some good suggestions of his own regarding what the sequences should be.

Stay Out of the Big Inning

Perhaps the most important rule of thumb for a pitcher is to stay out of the big inning. A single big inning of scoring often decides the outcome of the game. Thus a pitcher must pitch his way out of situations which present the opportunity for a lot of runs to be scored. Or better still, avoid them entirely.

This principle has led to the philosophy of giving up the run but get the out early in a game. Also, minimize walks by forcing the batter to hit his way on base. In a bunt situation, take the out, even if it advances the runner a base. In all of these circumstances the goal is to keep your team in the game, even at the expense of surrendering a run.

This will often happen when there's a base runner on third. Often the pitcher will focus too much on preventing this runner from scoring, so he'll try to pick him off or just hold him there with a couple of throws to the base. Even if this doesn't produce a wild throw, the pitcher's attention has been drawn away from his number one priority: the batter. This prevents quality pitches and usually a walk or base hit will result. Now he's gotten himself into a potential big inning. Remember, the game can sometimes be over by the third inning. Don't let this happen to your son.

Pitch to Bunters

A great many youth ball coaches teach their pitchers to defend against the bunt in the wrong way. In order to properly execute a bunt, the bottom of the bat should make contact with the top of the ball and direct it in a specific direction. So coaches tell their pitchers, "When you see the hitter square to bunt, throw a high pitch." If a batter insists on attempting to bunt the ball, it is usually popped up or fouled off. This would be a desirable result, except for one thing: very few pitchers can actually keep a high pitch in the strike zone. Too often the ball sails far too high out of the strike zone and the batter simply pulls back, away from attempting any contact. Repeating this strategy on the next pitch usually leads to a second called ball. Now the pitcher is really behind in the count and a solid hit or a walk often follows because now the pitcher has to throw a strike. And the batter knows it. Pitching high in the strike zone is not a sound strategy for youth ball.

Even at higher levels, this strategy is of dubious value. Many seasoned pitchers have difficulty adjusting their delivery just as they see the batter square to bunt. Thus the better tactic is to simply throw the original pitch. Let the hitter give himself up to move the runner over. The key is to get the out. That runner may eventually score, but this is by no means guaranteed. However, what is assured is that by taking the out, your son has moved a huge step closer to avoiding a big inning. This is key to long term success. Besides, not many players execute the bunt very well today. It's almost a lost art. Your son might still get a pop-up, fouled ball, or simply a missed attempt, for a strike.

With a Man on Base, Keep Pitching

When a batter gets to first safely, too often the disposition of the pitcher changes. Suddenly, one senses a feeling of urgency. Not knowing how to properly deal with the runner, fear usually takes over. Repeatedly looking over, stepping off, and attempting to pick off the runner usually produces only one result: the runner gets to walk to second base because the batter just got a free pass to first.

Too few pitchers understand the term *pick-off.* In fact, the word is misleading because of all the times the ball is thrown over, seldom, if ever, is the runner actually picked off any base. Stepping off, glancing over, and the occasional pick-off throw are in fact not intended to actually pick off the runner. These actions are executed for another reason. They are purely attempts to keep the runner close to the bag in order to prevent his taking an extra base or scoring on a single.

With this knowledge your son should govern his behavior accordingly. First, get rid of the fear of being unable to pick him off. Second, he should realize that a couple of looks over or just a step off is all that he may need to do in order to keep the runner close. And finally, and most importantly, his focus and main priority is the batter. If he worries too much about the runner, he's going to lose the hitter. Your son must concentrate on throwing a quality pitch. A preoccupation with the runner is one of the primary reasons for a big inning.

Greg Maddux explains his approach to the base runner this way: "I don't care if the guy runs on me. A guy can reach first, and I'll get one out. He can steal second, and I'll get another out. He can move up one more base, but I'll get the third out before he scores."

RECOMMENDED READING

The Mind Gym, Gary Mack, David Casstevens
The Mental Game of Baseball, H.A. Dorfman, Karl Kuehl
Play Baseball the Ripken Way, Cal Ripken Jr. and Bill Ripken, Larry Burke
Coaching Pitchers, Joe "Spanky" McFarland
Nolan Ryan's Pitcher's Bible, Nolan Ryan and Tom House
Think Better Baseball, Bob Cluck
The Pitching Edge, Tom House
Guide to Big League Pitching, Al Widmar

CHAPTER 2
PITCHING STRATEGIES - TACTICS AND ADJUSTMENTS

Tactics

This chapter concerns itself with more specific situations that will arise during the game. It will provide your son with a way to approach these situations such as recognizing the hitting faults and weaknesses of the batter in front of him.

Your son will have to constantly make adjustments throughout the game. Sometimes it will be as a result of one of his pitches not working or, in other instances, it will arise because the batters have adjusted to your son, or they are simply stealing signs. Knowing how to adapt to these occurrences will help maintain your son's record of success.

Strategy Determines Tactics

Strategy and Individual Sports

It is pretty well accepted in the world of sports that the strategy you choose determines for you what tactics which can then be employed. By and large, tactics must match up with the proper strategy. For example, in the one-on-one competition of boxing: before the October 1974 "Rumble in the Jungle" held in Kinshasa, Zaire, Muhammad Ali needed a clear strategy if he was going to survive the intensity of punishment "Big George" Foreman intended to hand out. At that time in the heavyweight division the most feared and powerful fighter was the champion George Foreman, because of his vicious attitude and the incredible punching power that went along with it. In 1993, one of his punches actually lifted then heavyweight champion Joe Frazier right off of the ground. Ali decided that he had to wear Foreman down before he could hurt him, but without also wearing himself out. He would then counterpunch and attack with less powerful but far quicker hands. Ali was one of many fighters, albeit usually at lower weight classes, who proved that the punch you didn't see coming was most often the one that knocked you out, not necessarily the one landed by a large but slow opponent. Pure power was not always the most lethal weapon. So Ali chose the tactic intentionally of allowing Foreman to tire himself out. After seven and a half rounds of clinching and lying on the ropes, while also allowing Foreman to unproductively wail away on Ali's arms and doing little serious damage, Ali decided now was the time to take advantage of Foreman's tiredness. Ali bounced off the ropes and threw quick, sharp punches. Before Foreman knew it, he had been counted out and lost his title. Ali's tactic has inappropriately become known as the "rope-a-dope" strategy but it proved a perfect fit of strategy and tactics.

Ali's strategy of tiring Foreman out led to his tactics of lying on the ropes, clinching and then when the time was right, retaliating with quick and lethal counter punches. But developing and implementing a new team strategy with its multiple tactics and personnel involved is much more complicated than the task Ali had to overcome.

Developing a Team Strategy and Tactics

In the 2009 National Football League season, Norv Turner, coach of the San Diego Chargers, also developed a strategy that he would effectively implement with tactics that appeared almost unstoppable. And the two were perfectly fit for success.

In prior years, San Diego had been known as a great running team led by the incomparable running talents of Ladanian Tomlinson (L.T.). Yet this slow time-consuming offense, which usually produced low scoring games, seemed capable of carrying the team only so far in the hunt for a Super Bowl championship. But Turner realized that he had another high-skill player whom he could also build his offense around, but in a completely different fashion. This player was quarterback Phillip Rivers. Turner also realized that if he was to go this route his strategy(ies) must change and his tactics would have to follow suit. So a radical shift occurred and not by any accident.

Years before, he had realized that he had the option of generating a high-powered offense that would simply score so many points that the opponent could not possibly keep up—a scoring machine if you like. But if he were to build this offensive juggernaut he would have to accumulate a particular set of players in order to make it work. A larger offensive line that could provide better pass protection than a lighter run-blocking line and larger wide receivers and tight ends would also be needed. In 2009, San Diego fully committed to the new strategy and the slow transition from a running team to a throwing team was complete. Now Rivers would use the tactics of having big tight ends and wide receivers running various slant routes over the middle of the field where, when hit, they could better absorb the punishment and hang on to the ball. More importantly, Phil Rivers with his strong and accurate arm could stretch the field with his tall, fast receivers and not worry about coverage. All he had to do was put the ball down the field and high into the air. This made it a jump ball situation for his tall receivers against mostly five-foot-nine-inch to five-foot-eleven-inch defenders. His taller athletic receivers almost always won these jump ball situations. This lengthening of the field then also opened up the underneath routes for other San Diego receivers (and running backs).

Norv Turner's offense illustrates the perfect mix of strategy with tactics. In fact, if you want to see when and how Turner made his choice to change offensive approaches just look at his draft choices and the year to year decline of L.T.'s running efficiencies since 2006. You'll see the same man at the top of his prime with diminishing stats, simply because a new strategy also demanded different tactics and L.T. was to pay the price with his diminished involvement in the offense.

But Youth Baseball is Different

Building a young pitcher who will also employ both strategies and tactics doesn't work in the same way as these professional athletes. In fact, this can usually be said for all youth sports. Utilizing professional offensive or defensive schemes is a mistake to ask of children. Similarly, demanding that youth ball players execute pro tactics is even more ill-advised. All adults, coaches, and parents alike have to realize that expecting a young player to replicate the strategies or tactics of a pro ball player is ridiculous. So lighten up and let's see if we can fly right.

A Youth Pitcher's Approach

Most young players are like a pitcher but usually with a lower skill set level. In youth ball, a pitcher determines his strategy by what he can physically do. Similarly, he develops his tactics by what he can actually throw.

For example: A pitcher may wish to throw 'hard to soft' (strategy) by mixing up a curveball and change-up with a dominating fastball (tactics). He may wish to throw the following sequence:

1. Fastball high inside
2. Curve low away
3. Fastball low inside
4. Changeup low inside

5. Fastball high at numbers

But your son may not have a curveball or perhaps even a change-up. This won't mean that there are no tactics at all available to him to use, just that the choices that the pros readily have at their disposal may not be available to him. So his choosing a strategy that requires the ability to execute specific tactics may not be available to him. The pros have already mastered executing passing skills, running, pitching, catching, etc. so their job is to adjust. Your son must first learn. Just remind him that an accurately thrown fastball still gives him tactical advantages when his pitch is thrown up, down, from side to side, and with more or less velocity.

The pitching skills taught in this book are done so in a progressive fashion that will permit your son to master skills needed to execute a tactic in the easiest and safest way possible. In turn this will now permit him to choose from among even more strategies that he can employ during the game.

When to Throw the Fastball

The "Book" suggests that the best times to throw the fastball are:

1. For a first pitch strike, low and away.
2. When you "need" a strike, when behind in counts (3-0, 3-1, 2-0, 2-1).

3. When the batter is expecting an off speed pitch (0-2).
4. With no one out and a runner at first and behind in the count.
5. When the batter has a slow reaction time.
6. Inside, on a batter who 'casts' with his swing.
7. Anytime a batter is overmatched by the pitcher.

When Not to Throw the Fastball

The fastball is the pitcher's meat-and-potatoes pitch. It should be thrown 75 to 80 percent of the time, so there are very few times when this pitch should not be used. Therefore, even when a batter is sitting on a fastball, often it must still be thrown. The trick is to put it in a location where the hitter is not looking for it.

When to Throw the Change-Up

The most common instances for when a change-up is recommended are:

1. When the hitter takes a big stride.
2. When the batter is considered a pull hitter.
3. When the hitter's front foot pulls out.
4. After the batter has pulled a fastball foul.

5. As a first pitch, when the batter is a first pitch fastball hitter.
6. Any time the hitter is sitting on a fastball, because the pitcher is behind in the count (2-0, 2-1, 3-1, 1-0).
7. When there are no outs, with a man on second and a right-handed hitter up.

When Not to Throw a Change-Up

In the following instances, the "Book" recommends when a change-up should not be thrown.

1. When the pitcher is ahead of the batter (unless the change-up has good movement).
2. When an opposite-field hitter is up, because he's used to waiting on the pitch.
3. When the hitter has two strikes (unless the change-up has good movement).
4. When there are fewer than two outs, with a man on first, and a left-handed hitter up.
5. When there are no outs, and a runner is on second, with a left-handed batter up.

When to Throw a Breaking Ball

The "Book" and many coaches agree that the following situations are ripe for throwing the breaking pitch.

1. When the hitter pulls his head away from the ball.
2. Any time the hitter is looking for a fastball (For instance, on the first pitch or on a count of 2-0, 2-1, or 1-0).
3. When a left-handed hitter who hits the ball to the opposite field is up to bat, because breaking balls will have him pull the ball.
4. Right after a previous breaking ball, because many hitters guess fastball after a breaking ball. Sometimes throwing three or four breaking balls is an effective tactic.

When Not to Throw a Breaking Ball

There is also general agreement on when not to throw a breaking pitch.

1. When the hitter is outmatched by the fastball. (Unless the breaking ball is thrown as an intentional ball).
2. When the hitter has a slow bat and is looking for off-speed pitches. (Unless the breaking ball is thrown as an intentional ball).

3. When the runner at first base is stealing, because the fastball gives the catcher a better chance to catch him. (Although sometimes a steal is inevitable and a breaking ball must be thrown).
4. To a left-handed hitter with no outs and a man on second base, because the batter intends to pull the ball.

A Caution

These recommendations of when or when not to throw certain pitches are simply guidelines. They must always be applied within the context of your son's abilities. For example, if he has good command of his change-up, then this can be an excellent 0-2 pitch. The batter is usually very aggressive and he certainly won't be expecting it. It is commonly used by my son as a strikeout pitch when batters were sitting fastball or even curve. So your son should always fit these guidelines within his own personal capabilities.

Get Ahead and Expand the Strike Zone

Statistics show that when a pitcher gets ***ahead in the count***, the probability of a batter getting on base declines. Batters feel the pressure of being ***behind in the count*** and so become less selective in their swings. Commonly coaches yell to them to "protect the strike zone" or "protect the plate" whenever the hitter has two strikes against him. This only encourages the batter to swing at a pitch, anywhere close to being called a strike. In essence, by the batter being behind in the count, the strike zone has been enlarged for the pitcher.

Similar thinking applies to the batter when the pitcher falls ***behind in the count***. Now the hitter knows that the pitcher can't waste pitches by picking at the corner. The batter also knows that strikes are needed and in order to get one, the hitter knows that the pitcher must throw something over the heart of the plate. In essence, now the strike zone has shrunk for the pitcher. So the batter can afford to be more selective and wait for ***his*** pitch.

Throw it Over the Middle Early

Normally you try not to throw pitches over the middle of the plate. The pitcher's locations are always on the outer third and hopefully with movement away to the corner. Pitches over the heart of the plate often get tagged and go for a ride. But not always. *When* they get tagged is important here.

Watch a major league team take batting practice before the game. These pitches are usually fastballs thrown over the middle of the plate in the high seventies or low eighties. Watch what happens to them. Almost every batter starts out chopping a few balls into the ground or fouling them back, or sky high, for easy fly outs. Until the batter finally finds his swing, after a few errant attempts, his swing is not yet in the groove. Since this is true of most batters at all age levels, use this information.

When the pitcher takes the mound, he too is still searching for his pinpoint accuracy. There can be many reasons for this lack of control. Perhaps he has a new grip, or the bullpen set up was not sixty feet six inches, or the mound is not steep enough or sometimes, it's too steep. There are many reasons why the pitcher is not entirely ready to bring his best stuff. But your son shouldn't panic. He has a big advantage that the hitters don't share.

Now your son must not fall behind on the first few batters and end up walking anyone. This could lead to a ***big inning*** early in the game. But remember the batting practice swing? Most hitters won't have their best swing and timing working yet. So have your son just aim for the middle of the plate for the first inning. As the inning moves along, your son will find more of his control, while the batter probably won't have discovered his in time. By the second inning, if your son's control has returned, have him go back to throwing at the outer third of the plate and even painting the corners. If there's any time that your son will get away with throwing over the middle of the plate, it'll be early in the first and second innings.

Away Early, In Late

Being able to pitch inside provides your son the tactic of pitching ***away early***, and ***in late***. By throwing strikes to the outside corner early in the count, the batter becomes worried about another pitch on the corner. Hitters tend to keep looking for this same pitch, which now makes them vulnerable to a fastball inside. They simply can't adjust in time to heat inside, when they're looking away. So get ahead early on the outside and then finish him off hard, inside.

When in Doubt, Stay Away

If your son has never seen a batter before or simply does not know what he should throw, then pitch away. By staying on the outside corner, with either heat or a breaking pitch, the batter has less of a chance of hitting this pitch hard.

Don't Let Their Best Hitter Beat You

Ideally, your son never wants to give a batter a free pass to first base. Too often those runners come back to hurt you and they often can be the start of a big inning. But in certain circumstances it may be smarter to chance walking the batter than giving him something to hit.

If your son's team is leading the game 7 -1 then he should go after every batter he faces. But if it's late in the game and your son is protecting a one run lead with a runner on base and their best hitter coming to bat, don't let him beat you with a solid hit. This batter is a known entity and a dangerous one at that, so don't give him anything to hit. Your son should pick up at the corners if he must, but stay away from the batter's strengths. If he walks, so be it. Your son should go after the next batter and throw a ground ball to his shortstop for a double play or the last out of the inning. But he should never let the obvious guy beat him with a big hit that you could see coming.

Even When Behind, Stay Aggressive

If your son is in a fastball count (per The Book) like 3-0 or 2-2, the batter will be expecting your son's best pitch, which is probably his fastball. Now your son could decide to *throw backwards* but perhaps his breaking stuff isn't working today. In fact, this may be the reason he's behind in the count. So what should he do? Throw the fastball that's expected but, with a surprise.

Most hitters are expecting a fastball so they're sitting on it. But most of them are expecting it right over the middle of the plate or on the outside corner, where they're limited in what they can do with it. Yet the one place few batters are expecting the next pitch is right in their power alley, inside. Since most batters won't be expecting this location, your son should draw a strike. But even for those batters who identify the pitch and adjust to this location, they still have to execute their swing early and accurately in order to do any damage. So if your son stays aggressive, he still has the edge.

Climb the Ladder

If a hitting coach had to give only one piece of advice to a batter, it might be for him to lay off of any high pitch. Even if it's in the strike zone. The reason is that the high pitches look so inviting and easy to hit. But a hitter needs to have very quick hands to make solid contact here. And most batters can't do it, so use this weakness.

When your son throws a high pitch and the batter swings, have him throw it again. Only this time *climb the ladder* and throw it just a little higher. Even if it's just out of the strike zone, the odds are that the batter will go after it. This is a particularly useful tactic for a hard-throwing pitcher.

Backing Up the Pitch

Backing up the pitch simply refers to throwing the same pitch you just threw, again. This isn't unusual when throwing the fastball, which is always being thrown back to back. But throwing another kind of pitch in succession, particularly to the same location, can be dangerous. Because a batter has just seen the curveball, he is now used to the velocity and break of this ball. If one throws it again, the pitcher risks throwing this pitch right over the fence.

But this is exactly why backing up a curveball with another one can be so effective. Most batters will assume that because throwing it again is so dangerous for a pitcher, he's going to sit on a fastball. A second curveball will often crumple the knees of the batter and get a strike called.

In the fifth game of the 2005 National League Championship Series, Cardinals pitcher, Chris Carpenter struck out the Astros'

Morgan Ensberg on six consecutive sinkers. Just imagine the thinking of this batter and pitcher match up. After backing up the first sinker, Morgan Ensberg knows he wasn't going to get another one, but he did. Now Ensberg knows for sure he's going to see something else, so he's not looking for the sinker. So Carpenter throws it once again. No way Carpenter's going to throw a sinker five times in a row, so Morgan is again looking for something different. So Carpenter throws the sinker, yet again. Even the next and final pitch of this match-up was a sinker thrown past Ensberg for a called third strike.

Carpenter's success in this match-up was based upon both surprise and a hard-thrown sinker. If a pitcher tries to mimic this feat with a slower-moving change-up or curve, it won't work. These pitches move slowly enough for the batter who is looking 'red' to adjust his swing down to a *softer* pitch. It is doubtful that a third curveball doesn't get hit hard. But with Carpenter's hard-moving sinker, it was more difficult to look for a breaking ball and then adjust up to the sinker's greater velocity. The combination of surprise, guts, and a hard-thrown ball got the out.

Backing up pitches can always be effective. Throwing the same pitch three times in a row can also be effective, but usually only with hard-thrown balls.

Fastball In and Out

A fastball in and then out is still the best combination of pitches. Moving the pitch up and down on the corners adds greater unpredictability. This sequence is effective even if your son is only throwing fastballs. If he can also add in breaking pitches to these locations, he will be even more effective. But remember, don't simply alternate inside and then outside. This is too predictable. Back up the pitch to the same location and then move it to the other side of the plate.

Pitchers with Movement Go Up and Down

Pitchers who have the ability to put lots of movement on their pitches often work the plate in and out, side to side. This is simply because they tend to play to their natural strength, which is a ball that moves side to side. There's nothing wrong with this, but your son can become known for this tendency, and teams will adjust.

So have your son throw off these batters by occasionally working ***up and down*** in the strike zone. Have him work a high fastball followed by a low strike. If this second pitch can be a breaking pitch (i.e. curve), he will not only have changed the batter's eye level for pitches, but the ***hard to soft*** combination will also throw off the hitter's timing.

If his control is good enough, have him pitch an entire inning high to low. Then the next inning, come back to his side-to-side strength, and then throw in just one high pitch with each batter. The batters won't have a clue what your son is going to throw next!

How Velocity Affects Strategy

Your son's high end velocity numbers can help him determine a strategy for the game. Generally, if a player cannot throw very hard, it is more important for him to be able to locate his pitches from side to side. This will help to keep the batter guessing and off balance.

If your son has high end velocity, then he must learn how to vary this speed and use a change-up. He won't be able to throw the ball past everyone. And, as he gets older, he'll be able to throw it past fewer and fewer batters.

Show Them Everything Early

If your son throws three pitches, he should show them all, early. This means throwing every pitch at least a couple of times in the first inning. But it doesn't mean throwing each pitch an equal amount of time. The key is for your son to establish in the mind of the batter that any one of three pitches may be coming. Even if the curve is only thrown two or three times in the first two innings, it will establish uncertainty in the mind of the hitter. This uncertainty can slow down his hand speed on all of your son's pitches.

Some coaches recommend holding back a pitch until the ***second time through*** the lineup. This can be effective, as a batter can often be fooled by a pitch that he had not yet seen. But it also means that the first time through the lineup, there is less uncertainty in the mind of the batter. As a consequence, with only two pitches being thrown, a batter may choose to sit on one of them. He has much less chance of guessing right if he knows your son can throw three pitches for strikes. Holding back a pitch until the second time through the order can be effective, but only if your son can get through the order the first time without being hit hard.

Get the First Batter Out

The most important batter of every inning is the first guy to bat. This player is the foundation for that inning's offense. He can set the tone and if he gets on base it will pick up the confidence of the entire team. So don't let him get on base.

Your son must be aggressive and go right after this hitter. Throw a first-pitch strike. Don't pick at the corners. Go right after him and force him to earn his way on base. Once your son gets him out, watch the rest of the opposing team lose its edge. If he can do this every inning, then he's guaranteed to have a lot of success.

Work Fast and Upset the Batter's Rhythm

By working fast your son will gain an advantage. Most batters prefer to take their time, think about what just happened and what approach they'll now take to the next pitch. But a pitcher can force a batter to stand in before he's ready to.

This is achieved by preparing a game plan, sharing it with the catcher and therefore lessening delays between pitches. The pitcher should not rush his delivery, only the time it takes him to step on to the rubber after he receives the ball back from his catcher. The hitter will feel naturally compelled to step back into the batter's box. If he doesn't, the umpire will move him along.

One of the other disadvantages for the batter is when a first-pitch strike is called and the pitcher quickly throws another. This unnerves a hitter, and a nervous hitter is always good for pitching success.

Pitching Ahead and Behind

The way your son chooses to pitch may depend upon whether his team is trailing by one run or is running away with the game. For example, if he's tried to throw his curveball during the first two innings but he can't find the plate with it, he'll probably abandon it and go to another pitch. But if he's ahead in the fourth inning by a big margin, then he may choose to see if his curve will work better now. So he may choose to try it again. But if it still isn't working and he walks a batter or gets hit hard, the damage isn't so bad. And his team is still ahead.

On the other hand, if his team is behind, tied, or just ahead by a run, your son won't have this option. The game will simply be too close for him to experiment or take too many chances. The Book dictates that when well ahead in the game a pitcher play loose and take some chances, perhaps even try out his new back-up curveball. But in tight games, it is recommended that your son plays more conservatively; still go after the batter, but don't throw the game away with needless mistakes.

When in Trouble, Go Soft

Occasionally, a pitcher will find that he can't get his pitches over the plate. He'll start walking batters, or alternatively, they'll start to hit him. Too often this pitcher will try to get out of this situation by just throwing the ball past the hitter. Usually this is a mistake. Seldom will your son have enough velocity, with accuracy, that will make this strategy work. Instead, have your son *throw soft*. Take something off of the fastball and have him hit his spots. Mix up the locations side to side, as well as up and down. In this way, your son can take advantage of the problem he's having.

Your son should realize that he's not the only one who knows that he's having problems. So do the batters. Often they can't wait to take their swings off of a pitcher in trouble. As a result they become *too aggressive*. They know the pitcher will try to get out of his situation by throwing hard fastballs, so they're all set to jump at the pitch. But if your son takes something off of his fastball, the batter usually just fouls the ball off or harmlessly flails away at the pitch. Even other off speed pitches like change-ups and curveballs will produce similar results when hitters are *too aggressive*.

Now, when he gets in trouble, remind him to throw soft and take advantage of the batter's own mistakes. Soon he'll be back in charge, and they'll be the ones in trouble.

Have a Short Memory

A pitcher must never let his last pitch interfere with his next one. If your son is hit hard, he must not let the fear of being hit again determine what he is about to throw. He may use the information about his last pitch, such as: the choice of pitch, its location, or its velocity and movement. He should then adjust his approach the next time he sees that batter. Making adjustments based on reason is always necessary, but he must never allow his adjustments to be the consequence of fear. He should forget and move on. He must always pitch aggressively to every batter.

Recognizing the Batter's Weakness

Most batters have natural weaknesses of one kind or another. They may not be able to hit inside pitches, or breaking balls away, or perhaps a fastball high in the strike zone. Often these weaknesses can be detected just by a pitcher watching how a batter sets up at the plate or how he executes his swing. Your son should know how to recognize a batter's weaknesses and how to take advantage of them.

The Batting Stance

The key to a hitter's success begins with his stance. Even the most successful major league player can have an unique stance, but even still, there is a consistency among all of them. Although they may begin their swing with very unique stances, just as they are about to swing the following is almost always the same:

> The stride foot is closed and planted directly back at the pitcher, front leg slightly bent, hands positioned just behind the rear shoulder. The entire body is cocked and ready to explode.

If this is the position that the batter has to arrive at, before he can execute the optimal swing, your son should consider how he can pitch to a batter who *cannot* get to this position efficiently. With this knowledge and your son's adjustment, he should be well armed to attack the batters. So your son should look for the following signs and throw the appropriate pitch.

No Flex in Stance

A batter who stands completely upright must drop into a flexed-knee position before he can rotate his body to swing the bat. This will produce a late swing, difficulty hitting a low strike, the barrel of the bat dropping before it makes contact, and his body will tend to spin away from the plate.

These difficulties will produce:

i) late swing – foul balls
ii) low strike – vulnerable low and especially inside
iii) dropped barrel – pop flies
iv) spinning off – vulnerable to pitches on outside corner

Hot Feet

This refers to a player who can't keep his feet still as the pitcher begins his delivery. This makes his balance problematic and weight shift difficult to execute as the ball approaches. The body weight tends to drop back disproportionately and also often results in an over-stride.

With poor timing, this batter will tend to jump at pitches, resulting in missed swings on balls high outside, as well as out of the strike zone. High end fastballs will also be hard to get to. So a mixture of *off speed* and high end *fastballs*, will give him lots of trouble.

Stance Too Wide

If the stance is too wide, the batter will not be able to rotate his hips quickly and smoothly. In an attempt to compensate for the lack of lower body motion, he will have to compensate with his upper body. This usually results in an *over-swing* and an uppercut in the bat's path to the ball.

High fastballs and *low breaking balls* are difficult to hit solidly.

Stance Too Narrow

If the batter's feet are inside of his shoulders' width, this narrow stance can compromise his stability. The batter often strides too far forward to compensate and regain his proper balance. Consequently, this over-adjustment means that his eyes will have difficulty reading the ball's rotational spin, location and velocity. This batter is always susceptible to a hard *fastball inside*.

Standing Too Far Away

The batter who stands too far away from the plate has difficulty hitting anything on the *outside edge*.

Standing Too Close

This batter can cover the outside edge of the plate but has difficulty with any pitch on the inside edge. He is constantly being jammed. Hard *fastballs inside* are literally impossible for him to contact solidly.

Standing Too Deep

The hitter who stands deep in the batter's box has more time to adjust to a hard fastball. But he becomes vulnerable to a breaking pitch that hits the strike zone at the front edge of the plate and then drops to the batter's ankles by the time it reaches him. The 12 – 6 *curveball* is particularly effective against this player.

Standing Too Far Forward

This batter is not fooled by the breaking pitch which just nicks the front edge of the plate and then drops dramatically out of the strike zone. But the hard fastball will get on him that much sooner. Unless he has exceptional hand speed, the *fastball* on the *inside edge* will overpower this batter.

Wrapping the Bat

Wrapping refers to a batter who holds the bat with his hands high and the barrel *wrapped*, or held behind his head, so that the end of the bat is pointing towards the third baseman (for a right-handed batter). This is commonly, and erroneously, thought to give the batter more power. But the point of contact is too far away from this set-up position, and the batter is often too late in getting to the ball.

A breaking ball will give the hitter time to unwrap and get the bat to the ball. A fastball will require the batter to have exceptional hand speed if he wants to make solid contact. The *inside fastball* requires him to start his swing even earlier. If your son can put the ball high and on the inside edge of the strike zone, the high starting point of the hands at the launch position makes this pitch unhittable.

One-Eyed Hitters

The best hitters see the ball with both eyes. If a batter has his head turned only halfway to the pitcher, then he can only see properly with his left or front eye. This means that identifying the pitch type and location must be done principally with just this eye. Any pitch with a lot of movement is very difficult to read. So ***curveballs*** are particularly effective against this opponent.

Pre-Swing Movement

Pre-swing movements are common amongst hitters. A short stride or tap of the front foot is a pre-swing motion. It is used by many batters as a timing device for their swing. It's used to set the hands in motion. Mark McGuire used such a technique. His arms would flap while waiting for the pitcher to begin his delivery. He used this to remind himself to keep the shoulders loose and the rear elbow down. Barry Bonds incorporated a hitch to initiate his hands to the ball. So many pre-swing motions can actually be useful techniques that assist a player in hitting the ball. But remember that these techniques are used by players with exceptional physical skills. A less talented player who mimics these pre-swing motions can find that these techniques can actually lead to problems in the player executing his swing properly. Your son should also be aware of them.

No Coil in the Stance

Batters coil their torso by about fifteen degrees from a straight line of shoulder to shoulder alignment to the pitcher. This slight turn, or closing the front shoulder, helps to give them more power. But it also does something else: it also helps the batter to get his hands moving.

So a batter with no upper-body coil usually has slower hands. ***Inside fastballs*** make it difficult for this hitter to get the bat head into the strike zone before the ball crosses the plate.

Stride Too Long

Players with exaggerated strides usually, and erroneously, believe that this will give them more power. But a batter with a long stride will have problems with his balance which will, in turn, actually result in less power.

Because a long stride causes the eye level to change, this batter has difficulty judging the type of pitch and its location. A long stride also requires this player to start his body motion sooner, in order to catch up to a hard fastball. So a *breaking pitch* like the *curveball* or off-speed *change-up* will have the batter out front *too soon* and *lunging* at the pitch.

Striding to the Ball

Many batters are erroneously taught to stride towards where they believe the ball will be pitched. This would mean that they should stride towards the outside of the plate (a closed-down position) on a pitch ***away*** and stride inwards towards the third base line (an opened-up position) or any pitch on the inside corner of the plate. But in reality there is not enough time for a batter to make this adjustment before the ball crosses the plate. Consequently, if a pitcher varies his stride direction and is occasionally successful, it's only because he *guessed right* on the pitch.

If a batter does not *stride square* (directly at the pitcher) look for a *dominant tendency*. If it is to *stride closed* then pitch *inside* and jam him. If it is to *stride open* then all pitches over the *outside* corner will be difficult to reach.

Batters Who Drift

A batter who uses a stride but doesn't land solidly with his torso upright and body weight held back is *drifting*. In fact, his body balance has been lost and his weight is shifted too far forward to execute a good swing.

This batter may look to be almost lunging at the ball. Consequently, *curveballs* and *change-ups* usually produce easy ground-ball outs.

Slow Striders

Any player who uses a stride, whether for increased power or only as a timing device, runs the risk of not getting the front foot planted in time. Batters with long strides are particularly susceptible to this problem. Your son should watch for this kind of hitter.

A *fastball* that follows two off-speed pitch pitches, like a change-up and then a curveball, usually leave this batter swinging late and wildly.

SWINGING WITH A BENT FRONT LEG

Whether a player is staying back on his rear leg to hit for power, or comes up on his front leg just to be a contact hitter, in both instances this front leg must lock up at the knee. If the player finishes his swing with his front leg bent, then he isn't getting any hip rotation or forward body motion into the ball. This will mean his hands and swing have slowed down.

Slow hands and bat to the ball can be taken advantage of with a hard *fastball inside*. Particularly if it follows a slower breaking pitch away.

HITCHING

A *hitch* occurs when a player *drops* his hands, perhaps only two or three inches, from his *launch position* prior to the release of the ball from the pitcher's hand. As the ball is delivered, the hands then move back up into the original launch position, and the swing is initiated forward.

Barry Bonds uses this pre-swing drop of the hands purely as a timing device to get his hands and arms moving, much the same way as a pitcher will use an overhead pump of the hands, just to get the body started and be loose. A hitch does ***not*** actually contribute something to the swing like power or quickness. In fact, the only successful batters who utilize a hitch must have extraordinary hand speed to begin with, simply because this drop of the hands and then recovery to the launch position all take valuable time away from reading the pitch and executing the swing.

Players with a hitch are vulnerable to *fastballs inside*. A pitch thrown inside over the plate at the hands is unhittable for all but those with exceptional hand speed. This is also Bonds' only weak spot.

Tucking the Hands

A player who holds his hands and forearm in tight to the body is *tucking*. Most players who tuck are trying to ensure that their hands get to the inside pitch in time. However, since tucking the hands and forearms actually deprives the batter of quickness, he will be prone to hitting weak flares and singles.

Since the batter tucks in anticipation of the inside pitch, throw outside and away. Fastballs have more energy than breaking pitches, so they help to give this batter a little more pop to an otherwise weak swing. Therefore, the pitcher should adjust and throw *breaking pitches* on the *outside* of the plate. If contact is made, it produces only a weakly hit ball.

Weight Transfer Through Hip Rotation

A proper weight transfer begins with about 60 percent of the batter's weight resting on the rear leg. The batter will begin to coil his upper body as the pitcher initiates his own delivery. When the pitcher's hand approaches the release point, the batter will initiate his stride, or knee lift, or foot tapping motion. The hands also load to the launch position, and then the weight-shift forward begins.

No Lower Body Rotation

If a batter does not use his lower body to generate power, this means that any hit ball will only go as far as the upper body will propel it. Unless the batter has exceptionally quick hands or is naturally very powerful, these hits will be popped up or hit for weak ground balls.

This batter should not be feared. A diet of *breaking pitches away* usually produce easy ground-ball outs.

Early Hip Rotation

Early hip rotation is common amongst very aggressive hitters. They simply need to wait a little longer on the ball and the problem would be solved. But until they do, their bat is getting into the strike zone before it should.

Mixing in *change-ups* and slow *breaking pitches* with *fastballs* will have the batter out in front of the pitch. Any ball contact will be with the wrists prematurely turned over. Again, the result will be pop flies and weak grounders.

Over Rotation or Spinning Off

The most aggressive batters are often guilty of over-rotating on pitches through the strike zone. They often spin off towards the third base line. This occurs because the batter is trying to ***pull*** everything over the fence and in doing so, he's ***opening up*** his front shoulder. His front shoulder is spinning off the plate, just like everything else.

If the front shoulder is pulling out prematurely, then this batter cannot reach to the outside edge of the plate. So your son should throw *inside* and off the plate (i.e. at the hands) occasionally, but live mostly on the *outside corner* with both *fastballs* and *breaking pitches.*

Lunging at the Ball

Attempting to counter the problem of pulling the front shoulder open, a player will sometimes try to hit over the ***front***

leg. The proper way to do this is by staying ***nose to toes***, which is perhaps exemplified best by players in the Asian baseball leagues. But too often, a player won't stay behind the front leg. Instead they commit too early and too far, out in front of the lead foot.

This batter will jump at the fastball with some success but have no success whatsoever against *change-ups* and *breaking pitches*. An early fastball inside makes these other off-speed pitches very effective. If he begins diving at the outside pitches, bust him back inside with another *fastball*.

High Front Shoulder – Low Rear Shoulder

In the ideal swing, the batter tries to keep his shoulders level to the ground as his weight shifts, and hands lead the bat to the ball on a shallow angle. But a player who begins his swing with his front shoulder raised will have a problem keeping the barrel of the bat level through the plane of contact. The longer the bat is in this contact plane, the more opportunity the batter will have to make solid contact. Instead, with this batter, the barrel will initially drop under this contact plane and result in the bat being pulled upwards to make contact with the ball. This is a problem also common to players who swing a bat that is too heavy for them.

This batter should be fed a diet of *fastballs* and *change-ups*. Controlling the bat will be difficult, so catching up to a fastball and hitting it solidly will be rare. The change-up will take advantage of his compensating to catch up to your son's fastball. Because the curveball may actually drop right into this batter's angle of bat swing, your son should not throw his deuce.

Batters Who Cast

The most common problem for young batters is casting. *Casting* occurs when the batter swings the bat and allows the barrel to lead his hands through the contact zone. This swing resembles someone casting a fishing rod.

Although this type of swing will permit the player to make contact with balls on the outer half of the plate, it is virtually impossible for such a batter to hit the *inside* pitch. Only if a hitter takes his *hands to the ball* first—leading the barrel of the bat—can he hit a pitch over the inside corner of the plate. So *fastballs inside* will easily eliminate this kind of batter.

High Pitch Swingers

Virtually everyone likes the high pitch. And why not? It looks so close and inviting, but good batters learn to lay off this pitch because the reality is, this pitch requires very quick hands to get the bat to the ball and make solid contact.

One of Jeremy's team mates saw this as his favorite pitch. So every swing in the on deck circle was an effort to hit the high pitch out of the ballpark. But this player didn't have exceptional hands, so he seldom hit his way on base.

If your son can identify a similar style hitter, he should move up and down in the strike zone. But he should then *climb the ladder* with *high fastballs*, just above the strike zone. It won't stop this batter from swinging. If contact is made, it'll usually produce an easy pop up. But most of the time it is an easy wildly swinging out.

Set Him Up First

The hitting faults described above can't all be detected while pitching off of the mound. Some, like the *closed-off stance,* will be obvious. But others, like the *late hip rotation*, will be more easily viewed from the bench. This is where you, your son's coaches, and other team pitchers can be very helpful in scouting the other team for weaknesses. During games when he's not pitching, your son should always be watching for these kinds of weaknesses. It will take some time to develop an educated eye for these batting traits, but the results will prove valuable in helping your son to *adjust* his pitching strategy.

Once your son has identified some of these hitting weaknesses, he will be able to adjust his pitch selection and location accordingly. But just knowing that the batter is vulnerable to a certain pitch doesn't mean that your son will be able to throw this *out pitch* three times in a row, because the hitter is trying to adjust, too. So your son's *out pitch* will have to be *set up* with another pitch first. It's after seeing this *set up pitch* that the out pitch becomes most effective. The following are a few suggestions for both the set up pitch and the out pitch, as well as the kind of situations in which they should be thrown.

Pitching to the Hitter's Weaknesses

Sometimes a batter's hitting habits will tip your son on how to pitch to him.

TABLE

HITTER'S HABITS	SETUP PITCH	OUT PITCH
Sweeping bat	Miss outside	FB in
Loop in Swing	Miss outside	FB in
Slow Bat	Miss outside	FB in
Hitch in Swing	Miss off-speed	FB up and in
Step in bucket	Miss FB in	Breaking ball away
Steps to ball	Breaking balls away	FB in
Lunges	Miss FB	Off-speed or FB up
1-2 count, on toes	Miss FB away	FB in
1-2 count, on heels	FB in	Away
Very aggressive	Same	Change speeds, nibble at the corners
Good FB hitter	Miss with FB	Breaking ball, change-up
Good CB hitter	Miss with CB	FB
2 strikes, goes opposite way	Miss with CB away	Bust FB in
Pulls everything	Miss in	Outside corner
Guess hitter	Mix up pitches	Mix up pitches
Stands away from plate and steps away from plate	Miss in	Outside corner
Stands away from plate and steps towards plate	Miss away	FB Inside corner
Stands back in batter's box	Miss FB away	CB
Stands forward in batter's box	Miss CB away	FB in
Golf swing	Miss low	Pitch up
Hits off front foot	CBs or FBs up	FB down
Front shoulder starts down	Low in zone	Up in zone
Front shoulder starts up	Up in zone	Low in zone
Tall, low ball hitters	FB inside	FB or off-speed away
Short, high ball hitters	Miss FB low	FB, climb ladder
Long Arms	Miss off-speed away	FB inside
Short Arms	Miss inside	Breaking pitch away
Upper arm/elbow at shoulder height or higher	Anything high inside	FB High Inside

Take a Second

Now that your son knows how a batter's stance or practice swings tell something about his strengths and weaknesses, your son should take a second or two with each batter. As he steps up on the rubber to take his catcher's signals, either before or after, he should look at the batter for a brief moment. See if the hitter is giving something away with how he stands or swings the bat. Don't take so long that it distracts your son from his first priority. But just a second or so, may help his execution of a quality pitch.

As the batter practices two or three swings, he's usually telling you something about where he wants you to throw the ball. Low-ball hitters practice their golf swings not a chest high swing. Likewise a high-ball hitter won't be practicing his shin-high swing. Use this exhibition. Does he cast or loop his bat? Are his hands tight to his chest and does he just extend his hands to that inside pitch area? Is he standing far away from the plate? Just take a quick second to see if he's tipping something about his swing.

And between pitches, as he's getting ready on the mound, have your son glance over to the on deck circle. Does he know the batter? Is he a hard hitting threat? Does he cast or take high swings with the bat? Your son shouldn't spend a lot of time with these assessments, but now and again, taking just a second can help your son enormously with his pitch selection.

Know the Pitch for the Count

The following are generally accepted rules from the "Book":

Breaking Pitch Counts 0-0, 1-2, 0-2

The batter is about to fall behind or be struck out, so he's nervous and usually aggressive. A breaking pitch usually buckles his knees.

Off-speed Counts 1-0, 2-0, 2-1

Since the pitcher is behind, most batters are looking fastball. Off-speed often gets the hitter to commit too soon.

0-0 Count

Although there may not be a lot of pressure on the hitter, batters at all levels usually hit under .200 in this count. The reason is because many coaches tell their players to take the first pitch just to see what the pitcher's got. Players who haven't been told to often hold back swinging for this reason anyway. So pitcher's throwing hard first-pitch strikes are very successful in this count.

2-0 Count

This is usually the hitter's most favorable count. At all levels of play the average is over .300 because the pitcher must throw a strike, and the batter knows it.

3-0 Count

A batter's success in this count is actually lower than in a 2-0 count, even though the pitcher is in a worse situation. The reason for this is coaching. Most coaches tell their batters to lay off of the next pitch, hoping that it will be a ball and his player will be given first base. Attack this lack of aggressiveness and have your son throw a quality pitch for a strike. It may be one of the safest pitches he'll throw all game.

0-2 vs. 0-2 Count

Most pitching coaches in an 0-2 count have their pitcher throw a set-up pitch somewhere out of the strike zone. Either a high fastball out of the zone or a breaking pitch away, even in the dirt, are most commonly recommended. The reasoning is that with the fastball the batter's eyes will be moved and he may even be brushed back off of the plate. The breaking pitch will slow down the batter's timing, even if he doesn't swing at the ball. The pitcher then should come back with a fastball low on the outside corner for a strike. By having moved his eyes up with a fastball or slowed down his timing with the curve, the hitter should now be vulnerable to something hard, low and away. The Book's only requirement for this strategy is that the set-up pitch must not be hittable.

Greg Maddux is not a fan of this strategy. He says:

> "The hitter is most vulnerable when you get him in an 0-2 bind. My goal is to take him out immediately. I'm going right after him, no fooling around with wasting a pitch up high or throwing one in the dirt. Why waste a pitch on 0-2? That's the most ridiculous thing I've seen in the game. People are scared to death of giving up a hit in 0-2 counts. It's the lowest batting average of any count. So when's the best time to get the hitter to swing at a pitch? You guessed it – 0-2."

Further in support of Maddux's position, since batters know that most pitchers are using a set-up pitch that won't be a strike, exactly how effective will that high fastball or bouncing curveball be? In fact, many hitters will *take* the next pitch, just because they know it's not going to be in the strike zone. So why not throw one there and surprise them?

On the other hand, most people don't share Maddux's command and pinpoint control. These players may need something to somehow help them upset the batter's timing. Your son should experiment and find what works best for him.

ANTICIPATE THE BATTER'S 0–2 APPROACH

For those pitchers who use the 0 – 2 count to set up their fourth pitch, don't forget that *batters anticipate* the *purpose pitch* by the pitcher. Whether the pitcher bounces a curveball or throws a high fastball for his third pitch, the knowledgeable batter commonly expects the next pitch to be on the outside corner (Whether it's a fastball or something soft. They'll usually sit red and simply adjust down to the curve or change-up). In fact, pitchers setting up the batter for the fourth pitch have become so commonplace that some coaches have taken to teaching their players to *take* the third pitch, and *sit on* the next pitch, low, on the outside corner. So don't be predictable.

Your son should consider throwing a fastball on the *inside half* of the plate. Not only will this often surprise the hitter, but even in situations where a batter is actually looking inside, he needs to get his bat going early in order to make good contact out in front of the plate. So if the hitter is at all *thinking outside*, he'll never catch up to the inside fastball in time. And if he's looking for an inside pitch, he still has to get his bat moving very early if he's going to do any damage.

Another 0-2 Alternative

Have the catcher give his sign and then hold his glove up high, as if to receive a pitch high, just out of the strike zone. Don't worry about the batter seeing the glove. In fact that's the whole point. Your son should then throw a high ball. Now repeat the signal and set the glove high again, just out of the strike zone. The batter will notice the arm motion and see the catcher setting up to receive another high pitch. Only this time, your son will throw a low pitch down and away, in the strike zone. If the batter is anticipating a high pitch at all, he won't be able to adjust quickly enough to the hard pitch low and away. Even the break from a slower curve can buckle his knees when he's looking high for something hard.

Lead-Off Hitters Reaching Base

At the major league level, when a lead-off hitter reaches first, he eventually scores just over 50 percent of the time. At youth league levels, this figure is closer to 75 percent. Therefore an early focus in every inning is a key to success.

Lead-Off Walks That Score

A 10-year collection of data from Division I schools illustrates the danger of walks.

Lead off walks that score	38%
Ninth inning walks that score	39%
Lead-off ninth inning walks that score	43%

These statistics illustrate why it is so important to minimize free passes.

Two Outs and Nobody On

Throw a first pitch strike to get ahead, especially if your team is leading. Force contact with your pitches. If he doesn't have power, stay low and over the plate. If he is a power hitter, even a home run won't do too much damage, so try to throw a strike low and away.

With First Base Open

With first base open there is no need to give in to the plate with a heavy hitter at bat. Throw a quality pitch to a corner and if you miss, he isn't hurting you.

A 2-2 Count – Stay Aggressive

In a 2-2 count, never throw a pitch that you'd be afraid to throw in a 3-2 count. If your son doesn't have confidence in a particular pitch, he shouldn't throw it in a 2-2 count. The odds are that it won't be a quality pitch. Now he's in a 3-2 situation but doesn't have the luxury of missing the strike zone. Plus, his target area has now shrunk, because he has to make a good pitch and the batter knows this. So in a 2-2 count, your son should throw a quality pitch with any one that he has confidence in. Stay aggressive.

Defending the Squeeze

The squeeze play is designed to score a run with the use of a good bunt (safety squeeze), or sometimes the runner breaks from third base even before contact is made with the ball (suicide squeeze). The recommended play is to throw the pitch into the opposite batter's box and hope that your catcher has recognized the runner is breaking for home. Alternatively, if your son is throwing a breaking pitch, he can continue to throw it and hope that no contact is made by the batter or the bunt is tipped foul.

However, the *non-book* strategy, proposed by many statisticians and sabermetricians, such as Bill James, point out that it is usually better to get the out and give up the run, unless it is late in a close game. Otherwise, the pitcher chances feeding into a *big inning* for the other team. And this would always be worse than allowing a single run to score.

Feed on Weak Hitters

Good pitchers feed on weak hitters. They always dominate the batters they ***should*** get out by pitching aggressively. Although pitchers should always be aggressive, against certain batters they must be even more aggressive. This includes the bottom third of the order, especially the number nine hitter. If a pitcher is required to hit for himself, more often than not there are other better hitters on the club. So go right at the opposing pitcher. If there's any time when your son can afford to miss his spot, it's with these guys. Force contact!

Even free swingers who lack discipline and are constantly aiming for the fences can be the focus of this increased aggressiveness, if his batting average is low. Your son must get the outs that he *should* get out, by going right after these hitters. Leave his battles for the better hitting batters.

Feed on Strong Hitters

Your son can take advantage of the *aggressive* batter's tendencies, just as well as he can the number nine hitter in the lineup. Every batter who hits in the three, four, or five spot is proud of this fact. This player knows that he's being relied upon by his team, indeed even expected, to knock in important runs. This will play on his mind. Your son must understand that this player doesn't just want to hit the ball. This player *needs* to hit the ball. So any of these players is likely to be more aggressive than he probably should be.

This batter is not only very susceptible to *change-ups* that follow a fastball, but usually he will try to hit the high *fastball*, even if it's out of the strike zone. In fact, if your son has missed with a couple of pitches off of the outside corner, a high chest-height fastball usually draws a swing of the bat. The batter will swing because after two pitches away that he had no chance at, finally here's something close enough to hit. Unfortunately for him, it's too close.

Most pitchers fear this part of the lineup. Instead, your son should learn to capitalize on the aggressiveness of these players and watch for ways to take advantage of it.

A Pitcher's Edge

What happens when the batter accurately anticipates the pitch? Your son must remember that he always has the edge and for one simple reason. Even when the hitter guesses right, he still has to execute properly.

Nolan Ryan used to start off batters he'd never pitched to before with fastballs, down and away. Even if someone recognized this pattern, the batter would still have to make contact at the right location and at the right time if he were to be successful. But if Ryan's ball had movement on it, this made the task even more challenging. And if the hitter was someone like Steve Sax, a notorious high fastball hitter, the adjustment was all that much more difficult to make.

So remind your son that even if he throws a bad pitch and misses his spot, the odds are still in his favor that the ball will be popped up or grounded to an infielder. This fact should help minimize any fear that he has of the batter.

Making Mechanical Adjustments

A pitcher must constantly be adjusting his approach to the game. With his strategy, he may start off pitching by the book and then in the third or fourth inning, he will start pitching backwards. Or, he starts off pitching hard to soft and then later just stays throwing everything hard until he is removed for the reliever. Strategy and tactics are dictated by the circumstances. But a pitcher may also have to make mechanical adjustments in a game.

Your son must always be monitoring his performance during the game. Seldom will all of his pitches be working the way he wants them to. When they do, he'll throw a no hitter that day. But if he has a problem in the middle of an inning, he'll likely have to make some adjustment in order to get out of the inning with minimal damage done. There are a few tips to remember.

When fixing anything, whether it be the failure to keep the ball down or up out of the dirt, he must make one adjustment at a time. Either extend the stride foot forward an inch or two, or reach farther at his release point. But don't do both at the same time. If he does and it results in another problem, he won't know that had he only used one correction, it would have done the trick perfectly.

Also, all successful adjustments are usually small ones. Whether it's moving the release point or a turn of the wrist, seldom will he have to make a large adjustment to what he is doing. He should remember that a small adjustment in his delivery becomes magnified as the ball moves to the plate. If the change isn't big enough, then make another small adjustment. Soon he'll have the pitch he's searching for. Therefore, it's seldom necessary to make more than a one-inch adjustment at a time.

The following table will identify the sorts of things that can go wrong with a pitch. These difficulties may be the result of a number of different mechanical problems. So your son can choose from a number of mechanical adjustments provided to correct his delivery.

PITCH	DIFFICULTY	PROBLEM	ADJUSTMENT
All pitches	High flat pitch	Elbow is too low at release	Ensure your son's hand fully opens to the palm away position at balance point 4
Fastball	High	Stride too short so release point is too early and high	Lengthen stride an inch or two
Fastball	High	Rushing, body rotates before arm in loaded position	Stay back at balance point 3, then come hard
Fastball	High	***Ragging off*** the pitch and not extending far enough	Reach and release
Fastball	High	Hard stride foot landing causes premature release	Land stride foot softly then lock up the leg
Fastball	High	A ***pancaking*** hand will result in a late release	Keep the fingers on top of the ball as the palm starts to square to the target
Fastball	High	A late snap release of the fingers will keep the ball up	Concentrate on an early finger snap with the cracking of the whip
Fastball	Low	Overthrowing generates a late release point	Stay loose and flexible
Fastball	Low	Over-striding lowers the release point	Adjust it back a bit
Fastball	Inside	Wrist dropping inside	Square palm up to target
Fastball	Inside	Short *closed* stride will generate early release point	Lengthen stride and land foot to 1 o'clock position
Fastball	Inside	Front shoulder opens up too soon generating an early release	Ensure stride foot is leading directly to home, then take the front side home as ***one piece***
Fastball	Inside	Front hip is opening too soon, thus opening up front shoulder	Take the left hip to the plate as the left foot strides

Fastball	Outside	Late release point	Adjust back
Fastball	Outside	Fingers off center like a cutter so it breaks away	Check grip
Fastball	Outside	Overthrowing up causes later release with stiff delivery	Stay loose and flexible
Fastball	Outside	A low arm slot can cause a sweeping motion and late release (late in game)	Correct arm up to normal slot
Fastball	Outside	A tilting head outside will pull the ball that way	Concentrate on taking the nose directly to the target
Fastball	No velocity	Overthrowing results in less flexibility and a loss of velocity	Stay loose and flexible
Fastball	No velocity	Pancaking hand (under the ball) at release point drains snap and velocity	Keep fingers on top of the ball and behind it with hand, squared to the plate
Fastball	No velocity	Too tight a grip deprives quickness to snap	Keep hand and wrist loose
Fastball	No velocity	Choking the ball too far back in the hand	Keep the ball gripped by the first finger pads
Fastball	No velocity	Slow snap of wrist at release	Concentrate on hand back then quick snap forward
Fastball	No velocity	Fingers don't snap the ball at release only the wrist	Ensure the two fingers snap down separately as well as the wrist ***cracking the whip***
Fastball	No velocity	Upper body slow rotation	Fire the hip when the left foot lands, pull with more explosive torso
Fastball	No velocity	Upper body doesn't flex down over front stride leg	Flex the torso by taking the chest to the target and down

Fastball	No velocity	Aiming the ball too much	Don't think about the pitching mechanics as it's thrown. Stay at 90 – 95% effort and just throw
Fastball	No velocity	Thinking about the pitch too much	Don't think about the pitching mechanics as it's thrown. Stay at 90 – 95% effort and just throw
Fastball	No velocity	***A chicken arm*** (***ragging off*** the arm) shortens the delivery and arm snap	Extend the arm and reach to the plate, then release. ***Stride long, pitch long***
Fastball	No velocity	Weight transfer too slow to home	Don't rush: Just stay back then take the front side home. Then, the backside home.
Curve	High	Casting over the top	When the hand reaches the ear, take it on a direct line to the target
Curve	High	Fingers under the ball	Stay on top of the ball with the fingers and the hand, and forearm at 90°
Curve	High	Ball held too tightly in hand	Stay as one piece, but loosen the grip near the release point
Curve	High	Hand speed too slow	Quicken the hand back, then ***handshake*** at the release point
Curve	High	Pulling front shoulder open prematurely, ball stays up	Take front hip to target closes the shoulder, then pull backside to home
Curve	Low	Elbow too low at release	Keep the elbow up and speed up the hand when it passes the ear

Curve	Low	Turning the doorknob	Keep fingers on top of the ball, and wrist firm during the chop
Curve	Low	Hooking wrist to ear slows release	Keep the hand and forearm at 90° at the ear
Curve	Low	Tight arm and shoulders slows down the delivery	Stay loose and flexible
Curve	Low	Slow hand speed drops the ball	Increase hand speed from ear to the chop
Curve	Low	If the body is *rushing* the hand never gets high enough at release point	Stay back at balance point #3, then bring the backside home
Circle Change-up	High	Too slow a delivery will leave it up	Maintain fastball arm speeds. ***Think fastball***
Circle Change-up	High	High release point	Reach and pull palm hard to ground faster
Circle Change-up	High	Too loose a grip	Keep the wrist and fingers loose but firm
Circle Change-up	High	Too deep a grip	Adjust ball forward on fingers pads
Circle Change-up	High	Throwing across the body because the stride is too closed off	Stride directly to home and land the foot pointing at 1 o'clock
Circle Change-up	High	Pulling down too early will generate a high release point	Reach to full extension into the release window – then pull.
Circle Change-up	Low	Guiding ball to target	Just throw it without thinking it through
Circle Change-up	Low	Too tight a grip will bury it	Stay loose but firm
Circle Change-up	Inside	Low arm slot	Maintain fastball arm slot
Circle Change-up	Inside	Wrist turns inside to body	Square wrist and palm to target
Circle Change-up	Inside	Wrist too loose, it will be up and in	Firm it up a bit, reach and pull

Circle Change-up	Outside	Holding ball too long	Think fastball and throw. Let the natural mechanics kick in
Circle Change-up	Outside	Stride too open at landing	Keep left hip to home as foot strides forward
Circle Change-up	Outside	Front shoulder flies open	Stay back at balance point #3, take left hip home then backside to target
Circle Change-up	Outside	Wrist turns outside away from body	Square wrist and palm to target

Who Decides on the Pitch?

The relationship between a pitcher and his catcher is vital to the outcome of a game. For this reason, a pitcher and catcher must develop a rapport for the calling of pitches. Before each game they must get together and talk about the opposing hitters, what pitches are working well today, what sequences a pitcher may wish to use, whether they should utilize *the Book* today or pitch *backwards*, and so on. But even with all of this preparation, at some point during the game a catcher will call for a pitch that the pitcher won't agree should be thrown. What should happen then? There are three different points of view.

Coach 'A' believes that the only way to develop a catcher is by letting him decide what to throw. This coach teaches that the catcher has a more objective view, can see the entire field behind the pitcher, and should be the leader on the field. The pitcher should trust in his catcher's judgment and only shake him off for another pitch, in a limited number of instances. I've known of a coach who gives his pitchers only three credits or shake-offs per game. After they're used up, the pitcher must throw whatever the catcher calls. Typically Coach 'A' types were themselves position players, not pitchers.

Coach 'B' is a coach who understands that to maximize a pitcher's aggressiveness, he must have confidence in the pitch he's about to throw. He must believe in it! Many of the pitches that are called by his catcher he will either agree with or at least trust that it's the right call. But some calls won't be right for him.

Coach 'B' will allow this pitcher to shake off his catcher until he gets the sign he's looking for. He will permit the pitcher to wait for the pitch that he will have the most confidence in throwing. If it turns out to be the wrong pitch, even then it'll afford your son the opportunity to learn and most probably realize that his catcher knows more about the game than he had thought. This kind of failure can actually help build trust between the two.

A third approach is used by Coach 'C,' who calls all the pitches from the bench. The pitch will be signaled to the catcher by a coach, sometimes with the help of a dummy signaler, to avoid the sign being stolen. The 'C' type coach believes that his knowledge and experience affords him the best vantage point for making the call. In addition to knowing the strengths and weakness of his pitcher, he may also know if the runners will be going, the style of hitter that's at bat, and any number of other things about the opponent.

This very hands-on approach also has very real disadvantages. The kind of coach who uses it is typically a micromanager all over the field. He wants to be involved in everything even when he has assistants. Although his involvement might help his team win, this kind of control never helps a player develop. The catcher never learns how to call games, nor handle his pitchers. Similarly the pitcher doesn't shake off his catcher's sign because he knows he's actually shaking off his coach. How many young pitchers have the courage to do that? So he never develops his own feel for the right pitch. Worse still, he's forced to throw pitches that he doesn't believe in. Pitchers for type 'C' coaches typically pitch more tentatively than other pitchers and progress less rapidly.

Your son must always be the final decision maker as to what pitch to throw. It will be the pitch that he has the most confidence in and will promote an aggressive approach to his game. If he's wrong, he'll learn from his mistake and then use this knowledge to become a better pitcher. It's well worth finding out before your son joins a team the kind of signal-calling philosophy the club employs.

Type C coaches also have a problem not shared with the other kinds of coaches. Because a coach is out in the open when signaling to his catcher it is clearly easier to steal signs from this location than when they are hidden by the catcher between his legs.

And finally, sometimes it's not difficult to steal signs at all. At a recent conference, a well-known coach, who lets his catchers call their own games, recounted an incident. A very successful high school coach called all the pitches from the bench in every game. This coach was also having serious problems with one of his players and reprimanded him sternly with a suspension. The next game the coach and his team got blasted out of a game by a team that they had already beaten badly earlier in the season. The reason why this team bounced back so strongly is because the suspended player told the other team the coaches' signals. It was just the player's way of getting even. Although this specific scenario won't occur often, it does illustrate the problem of preventing leaks of a team's signals, for whatever reason.

Signals for a Stubborn Catcher

Ideally the pitcher and catcher, are on the same page when calling pitches. But this isn't always the case. If a pitcher wants to throw a quality pitch, he must believe in it. Only he will know if the new ball he's been given by the umpire is so slippery that his change-up or curveball are slipping out of his hand. If he doesn't want to throw a pitch because he doesn't trust it, he shouldn't. Because it's very doubtful that he will be successful with it.

In one game Jeremy wanted to throw a fastball to the batter but his catcher signaled for a curve. He shook it off. The catcher signaled for a curve. He shook it off. The catcher signaled for a change-up. Another shake-off. The catcher then signaled for the curve, again. Shake off. Jeremy then sees another change-up signaled. Another shake off. This simply can't continue. It destroys both a pitcher's rhythm as well as his focus.

Some jokingly suggest that the second time the curve or change-up is flashed, without first showing the sign for fastball, the pitcher should just throw the fastball. This will shake up the catcher and end this "Bull Durham" attitude. But this is a dangerous tactic to ever use, particularly when a much safer and simple alternative way of resolving the dispute is available. Your son should just use the glove swipe approach.

The Glove Swipe Signal

The ***glove swipe*** technique is effective, simple and versatile. If a pitcher has three pitches, a fastball, curve and change-up, then the signals for these pitches are typically called by flashing one finger, two, and three, respectively. If your son ends up in a similar situation to the one Jeremy faced, when he wanted to throw a fastball, this is what he should do when he sees the curveball sign for the second time. Have him take his glove and swipe his glove-side shoulder, twice. Then immediately start his wind-up and throw.

The number of times your son swipes his shoulder, signals to his catcher how many time he must *add one* to the original sign that was signaled. Because this is what he's about to throw. For example, if your son wants the change-up and all his catcher flashes is the curve, then swipe the shoulder once and throw. Adding one to the curve means that your adding one finger to the original two-finger sign that was flashed by the catcher. Two plus one equals three. And three fingers is the sign for the change-up.

If your son swipes twice, this means *add two*. But since he only throws three pitches, there is no fourth pitch to throw. Instead, the pitcher and catcher know that this means that, after the change-up (three fingers) the *rotation begins over* again. So the second swipe will actually bring up the fastball as the designated pitch. If your son actually swiped *three* times this would mean one for the change, the second swipe for the fastball and the third swipe would bring up the curve again. Of course this would never happen, but you can see how this *swiping system* works.

Swipe, Then Throw

A couple of points are worth mentioning. Since the *swipe technique* is intended to end the discussion between the catcher and pitcher, your son must immediately begin his delivery after swiping his shoulder with his glove. Don't let him delay, because this would allow the catcher to start signaling all over again, if he didn't like your son's choice of pitch.

Second, the glove should swipe the glove-side shoulder, not the throwing side shoulder. From the wind-up the catcher will be able to clearly see the throwing side shoulder, to identify the number of swipes. But when your son sets up from the stretch, the catcher no longer has a clear view of the throwing shoulder and may miss the count. So by swiping the glove-side shoulder, the catcher will always be able to clearly see and count the number of swipes.

Don't worry about this swiping technique giving away the pitch. Unless the opposing team also identifies the original sign that was flashed, they won't be able to recognize whether the final decision by your son has moved from a change-up to a curve, or a fastball to a change-up.

Swipe for Location Too

The glove swipe can also be used to identify the location of the next pitch. If your son throws both a fastball and a sinker, these are both types of ***fastballs***. Let's say the catcher calls for a fastball *away* but your son wants to throw a sinker *in*. No problem. Rather than force the catcher to go through his signals again and call a fastball inside, your son only needs to swipe his glove side near the waist and down to the top of his left thigh.

The *downward swipe* tells his catcher that the ball will be thrown to the *opposite side* than that which was called for by the original sign. The type of pitch doesn't change. Only it's location. So if the catcher calls for a curveball or the *outside* corner, the downward swipe simply tells the catcher that your son intends to throw the curve *inside*.

Glove Swipe, Advantages and Use

The glove swiping technique gives your son a way of ending endless debates about pitch selection. It also permits him to make minor adjustments to location quickly. And if he suspects that the other team is stealing his catcher's signs, then he can swipe his shoulder to change pitches or swipe his leg to move location. This will usually make stealing signs, then also looking for swipes, too complex for opposing teams. It's made even more difficult when a pitcher and catcher agree that the swipes mean *subtract* by one, or for the downward swipe, *leave location alone*.

The Bullpen Warm-Up

Many young players overvalue their performance in the bullpen. Whether this pitcher is a starter or comes in for relief, a bullpen performance should not dictate how your son pitches in the game. Too often a young pitcher can't hit the plate with one of his pitches in the bullpen, let alone throw it on the corners. So he assumes that he won't have that pitch working that day and abandons it for the game. This is a mistake.

Bullpen sessions are first and foremost, just a way to warm-up the body. Then it becomes a way to get familiar with the pitches. A player plays catch using his different grips just to get the feel of the ball for that pitch. After a little long toss, many pitchers throw off of level ground to a catcher, just working on the mechanics of the body, and not on pitch location. His velocity is at about sixty percent and he then cycles through his pitches. Typically after this, he'll move to a mound for a set, focusing on locating the center of the plate. Either the latter half of this set, or during an entirely separate set, he will move his pitches to the corners. The pitches will then be thrown in combination of fastball – change up – fastball – curve – curve – fastball – change up – etc., while working side to side. Only the last five to ten pitches will be thrown at game velocity. Your son must never leave his best pitches in the bullpen. Cy Young award winner, Pat Hentgen, says that he always seemed to throw 42 or 43 pitches in the pen, no matter how he adjusted his warm-up. This is about average for most major leaguers.

So as you can see, a bullpen session should never be mistaken for how well your son may actually execute a pitch that day. Nolan Ryan observed, "Never put too much stock in how you throw in the bullpen; loosening up your arm is not the same as pitching in a game."

Sample Warm-Up and Bull Pen Session for 15-year-old

I Warm-Up

- Easy jog of field, or jumping jacks, or skipping, etc. for 5 minutes
- Flush the blood and oxygen through the muscles
- Just get loose

II Stretching

- Stretch 30 – 45 seconds each, time permitting
- Lower Body in order: calves – Achilles tendon – ham strings (static and ballistic) – groin (static and ballistic) – glutes – quads – lower back – sides hip flexors – IT bands
- Upper Body in order: shoulders – anterior, lateral, posterior (all static and ballistic) – traps – rotators – upper back – biceps – triceps – chest – forearm (back and front)

III Warm-Up Catch

- Start with fastball grip
- Start close then gradually lengthen distance to 60 – 70 feet
- Nice easy fluid motion
- Focus on getting loose, no particular mechanical adjustments unless really needed
- Now use each grip of pitch to be used that day, curve, change, etc.
- Get used to the delivery, grip, and release

IV Long Toss

- Slowly lengthen the distance from 60 feet
- Extend to up to 200 – 215 feet
- Don't throw all out until the final distance is achieved
- Only throw 3 – 7 at maximum effort
- Then work way back in to 60 feet

V Level Ground Catch

- From the set position
- From 60 feet, focus on grip, mechanics and release
- Think about mechanics
- Cycle through the pitches, curves, sinkers, changes, etc., 3 – 5 each

VI Mound Pitching

- From the set position at 70 – 75%
- Again cycle through the pitches
- Focus on hitting the center of the plate
- Don't think about mechanics
- Just pitch, 10 – 12 pitches

VII Mound Pitching (or Second Half of Prior Set)

- From the set
- Focus on halves of the plate
- Move the ball side to side
- From the wind-up, repeat above
- 10 – 15 pitches

VIII Final Mound Pitching

- From set and wind-up
- Throw combinations
    - fastball – change-up
    - fastball – curve
    - fastball – sinker
    - change-up – curve, etc.
- Locate all
- End with good hard pitches, 5 – 10
- 15 – 25 pitches

Total pitches = 35 – 50

Then go talk to the catcher about the game plan.

Don't Lose to Bad Weather

Many young pitchers are successful when pitching without any wind, on dry ground, with a cloudless sky, and the sun at their back. But when the wind starts to blow, the mound conditions are poor, and perhaps there's even just a little rain, then they can't find the strike zone. Don't let your son fall victim to these conditions.

Inevitably your son will also end up having to throw a ball that doesn't feel quite right. The umpires don't have to give him another one. Or, he'll pitch from a mound that slopes differently from the one he's used to. He can't let these and other conditions affect his performance. Besides developing a mental toughness that comes from cultivating a strong sense of confidence in himself, he can do something else to strengthen his confidence in his ability to always be able to pitch.

Have your son occasionally practice in poor conditions. If you know where there's a poorly kept mound, occasionally have him throw off of it. If it starts to drizzle, don't immediately run for the dugout. Pitch through it. And use both new and really beat up balls in his pitching practices. Don't just use the slightly worn ball that always gives him a good grip and feel for his pitches. If he can do these things, then when similar conditions throw off the opposing pitcher during a game, your son will feel all that more confident when it's his turn to take the mound. And we all know that confidence breeds success.

A Pitcher's Ingenuity

But what if an umpire hands your son a new ball to start the game and it's so slippery he just can't control it? Most umpires won't do this but if it's the only ball he has, your son must adjust. The rules of baseball don't permit defacing the ball or applying any substance to them, although major league balls are worked-in by the umpires before the game with a special kind of dirt to ensure that they can be gripped by the pitcher.

It's surprising how in circumstances like this, how many experienced pitchers suddenly become clumsy. Often an otherwise well-coordinated pitcher who, while turning away from home plate and as he rotates the ball in his hands to work it in, accidentally drops the ball. It falls in the dirt behind the rubber and as the pitcher picks it up, it gets a little dirty. Some pitchers even accidentally get their throwing hand dirty. So when they recover the ball and again rub it down, it now looks like anything but a brand-new ball. It even seems easier to grip. So the next time your son is handed a new ball he should just make sure that he isn't so clumsy.

Mix it Up and Learn

All of the principles, tactics and specific strategies just mentioned should be interpreted flexibly. If your son has yet to really master his control, he must take and use from these pages only that which he can execute. In addition, if he has a high end fastball, then contrary to the philosophy of only pitching inside when ahead in the count, sometimes he can go inside sooner with his heat. But only sometimes. Moreover, if your son becomes recognized for only *pitching by the book* or *pitching backwards*, then his predictability will probably get him into trouble. So your son must also be willing to learn from his mistakes.

In a high school league game, Jeremy started the hitter off with his lowest level fastball (he has three levels) which the batter fouled off. He then threw a curveball for a strike. Now ahead in the count 0-2, he made a mistake. He threw a change-up which was up higher than it should have been, so the batter smiled and went for a jog around the infield.

The problem with this pitch was not so much that it was too high in the zone, but rather that, after just throwing two *soft pitches*, he threw another one. What he needed here was an increase in velocity to keep the batter off balance. But a third soft pitch allowed the batter to easily time it and give it a ride. After reviewing this pitch sequence following the game, Jeremy recognized the danger that this sequence of pitches presented, and will be cautious about ever using it again.

So remind your son to choose only those pitching strategies and techniques that his abilities permit him to execute. Then, continuously mix them up so as not to become predictable. And finally, learn from everything he does. Even the bad things. This will be a sure recipe for his long term success.

RECOMMENDED READING

The Mental ABC's of Pitching, H.A. Dorfman
Heads Up Baseball, Tom Ravizza, Ken Hanson
Why Johnny Hates Baseball, Fred Engh
Will You Still Love Me if I Don't Win?, Christopher Anderson
101 Ways to be a Terrific Sports Parent, Joel Fish
Sports Parenting Edge, Rick Wolff
Just Let the Kids Play, Bob Bigelow, Tom Moroney, Linda Hall

CHAPTER 3
HOLDING RUNNERS AND PICKOFF MOVES

An important part of a pitcher's performance involves preventing a batter from stealing a base once he gets on. Often this involves pickoff moves. But in order to execute this well, your son must first understand what he is trying to accomplish.

The Purpose of Pickoff Moves

The term pickoff move is misleading because the purpose of these various types of moves is not to actually pick off the runner. If it was, then someone should be fired. Because seldom does anyone, at any level of ball, ever actually pick the runner off of the base. But this is okay because there is another purpose for the pickoff play.

Contrary to public opinion, all of the moves a pitcher uses to confuse the runner are intended to simply upset his timing and slow him down. A pitcher's actual goals are to:

1) prevent the runner from taking an extra base on a hit,
2) prevent the runner from scoring on any long ball hit, and
3) reduce the chances of his stealing.

If a pitcher cab actually catch the runner off the base, then this should be seen as a bonus. Leo Mazzone explains that when you're holding runners on at first or second, you're trying to keep them from taking the extra base. And, "…throwing over to the first baseman time after time, after time, is joke."

Coach Ron Polk also teaches, "A pickoff play is successful even if there is no out made on the runner. The primary area of concern is for the defense to be able to control the baserunner's movement."

Proper Focus

What Mazzone goes on to emphasize is that the pitcher's primary focus must always be the batter, although some effort must in fact be taken to try to keep the running game in check. However, your son would be wise to remember that *holding the runner* is intended to only slow the running game down. As we now appreciate that the purpose of the pickoff moves, your son shouldn't be focusing on trying to get the out on the base paths. The only out he must really focus on is standing at home plate. Mazzone puts it this way: "… You have to remain firm in your conviction that you must continue to pitch as if there is no one on base … even if the bases are loaded." And, "The priority is always the hitter."

Greg Maddux has also put holding runners and attempting pickoff moves in the proper perspective: "I don't care if the guy runs on me. A guy can reach first and I'll get one out. He can steal second and I'll get a second guy out. He can move up one more base, but I'll get that third out before he scores."

So if your son can just slow down the opposition's running game, then he's done his job. Understanding that his goal is simply to *hold runners* close to the base, your son should now focus on the different tools he can use to accomplish this. These will include an assortment of feints, as well as actual throws to the various bases.

Vary the Set Time

With one exception (see later), a pitcher will pitch out of *the stretch* or form the *set position*, whenever a runner is on base. This will shorten the pitcher's delivery to the plate and thereby limit the time a base runner has to get to the next bag. But a good baserunner will try to time how long a pitcher stands with his hands together before he begins his delivery. So vary this time.

Some coaches have the pitcher begin his delivery after a count of two on this pitch and three or four on the next. The University of Michigan players are told to sing part of a song to themselves and then throw. On the next pitch, sing the same song in their head but start the delivery at a different place in the song. Using this *song lyrics* technique pretty much ensure that the pitcher's time will vary from pitch to pitch.

Step Off

Have your son occasionally step off of the rubber and then look over the base. Varying the length of delivery and then adding the occasional step off is a good way to cause a runner to hesitate. If he hesitates, he probably won't go.

Use a Slide Step

A slide step is simply an abbreviated way of delivering the pitch to the plate. A player will either shorten or entirely eliminate the leg lift from his delivery. This up, down and stride to the plate is now only perhaps a leg lift of three to four inches and then stride home. Some pitchers may even shorten the length of the foot strides to home. This abbreviated motion means the pitcher is quicker with the ball to the plate, giving the runner less time to adjust. Again, he may hesitate and lose his opportunity.

Although this technique can work to hold the runner, most young pitchers don't pitch well while using it. The problem is that the arm opening to the *palm away* position is normally timed to the leg lift and stride. So that when the stride foot hits the ground, the ball is in the *loaded position*. However when the leg lift is eliminated, the stride foot lands before the ball is fully loaded to *second base*. Now when the shoulders rotate, as the stride foot lands, the arm is too low and dragged through a low and improper arm slot. The resulting premature release of the ball causes the pitch to run high, out of the strike zone. After four of these pitches the pitcher will now have two runners on base. This delivery can also cause an injury to the low elbow, as well as the front of the shoulder, resulting from pulling the arm forward.

If your son can't speed up his hand separation to match the quicker stride motion, he should probably avoid this technique. However, there is a minor adjustment that he could make that may overcome the problem created by a shorter stride motion. If your son naturally holds his hands closer to his waist while in the set position, have him adjust this. Ask him to hold his hands higher, at this chest level.

Now when he separates them to the palm-away position, his hand will have less distance to travel. Consequently, his hand will now arrive at the loaded position just in time to be taken home. However, if he already begins his motion with his hands at the chest level, this adjustment is unavailable to him. This young player would be wise to simply ignore the slide step, and use the other techniques mentioned in this chapter for holding runners.

Throw Fastballs

Runners like to run when slower off-speed pitches are thrown (curves, change-ups). A pitcher who can throw hard can use this pitch to keep the runner on the base. And even when they try to steal, the sooner a pitch that gets to home, the easier it will be for the catcher to throw out the baserunners.

However, smart base stealers know that this technique is often employed by hard throwers. So they sit, looking for the fast ball. This strategy occasionally leads to hard hit balls.

Make a Quick Pitch

The kind of quick pitch referred to here is on the baserunner, not the batter. If your son quick-pitches a batter, he'll be called for a balk. But there's nothing wrong with quick pitching the runner.

Like a batter, runners usually go through a set process before they're ready to steal. He'll often measure off his primary lead, then his normal secondary lead and then adjust to this particular pitcher. He'll drop into his stance and get his hands and arms where he wants them. Then he'll sharpen his focus to look for a stride foot movement, or some particular area of the body that tells him to go. Well don't let this happen so casually. Upset his preparations.

A lot of good baserunners are disciplined when leaving the bag but much less so in going back to it. Watch the runner and if he hasn't stretched out his lead, throw the pitch. Alternatively, if your son has just stepped off or taken a long look over, the runner has probably retreated to the base. A quick pitch before he can re-set will often hold him at the bag.

Throw to the Bag

Ensure that the runner takes your son seriously by having him throw to the base. These *pick-off moves* will be described in the following section and are a little more complex than one might imagine. So add in these pick-off throws to slow him down.

Put Them All Together

No one of these techniques will work all of the time. The most successful approach is to combine the use of all of these techniques. Mix in looking over, stepping off, quick pitches, and varying his pitching tempo with the occasional throw to the bag. This will give the baserunner more to think about and usually slow him down.

Don't Tip the Pitch

If a runner is going to steal a base, ideally he wants to run on your son's curveball or change-up, not his fastball. These off-speed pitches will give him an advantage because they get to the plate slower than the fastball. The curve is your son's slowest pitch and the best to run on. Unfortunately for him, often the baserunner will know that it's about to be thrown.

At higher age levels, a pitcher's fastball can have a lot of giddy-up. So a catcher will not only want to know when your son's going to throw but, he also wants to know its location. A catcher doesn't want to be chasing a fastball to a corner that he didn't anticipate or dodging one inside, when he was expecting it outside. It's a good way to get hurt. So a catcher will first signal for this particular pitch and then its location.

But a curveball is different. Even at the Major League level, many pitchers find it difficult to spot this pitch. Therefore, the catcher usually only flashes a sign for the deuce, sets up in the middle of the plate, and then reacts to the location of the ball's break. And that's when a smart baserunner will take off.

If the baserunner sees *two signals* flashed by the catcher, he *knows* that the pitch is the fastball, with its location sign. But if he sees only one signal, then he knows that an off-speed pitch is coming. And since more pitchers throw a curve than they do a change-up, he knows that your son is about to throw his curveball. So he'll be off running as soon as your son starts his motion home.

Since the catcher must know exactly where your son intends to throw his fastball, this sign must be flashed. But there are a couple of ways to prevent a runner from counting the signals and running off of them. The best way is to have the catcher flash both the fastball and its location with one signal. If the ball is to be thrown inside, then the catcher shows his *pointer* finger pointing towards the inside of his left thigh. For a fastball *outside* he flashes his *baby* finger pointing towards his right thigh. This simple gesture to either side for the fastball, should mask when a single sign for the curveball is flashed.

But what happens if your son wants to throw a fastball, but to the other side than was indicated by his catcher? He still won't have to flash two signs. Instead your son need only swipe his left hip with his glove and the catcher will know that the called location is being moved to the opposite side of the plate. Runners don't have time to watch both the catcher and the pitcher's reaction and swipe. Your son's signals for his curveball should still be safe.

Get a Feel for the Runner

Good hitters develop a feel for some pitchers. Similarly a pitcher will get a feel for certain batters. This is why some pitchers own certain hitters. They have a sense for what the batter wants to do and so they pitch away from this plan.

Your son should try to develop a feel for baserunners. This means watching them very closely, particularly when sitting on the bench. Do they have any habits that may give away their intention to steal? Does their stance change when they're faking to go and when they actually try to steal a base? Be aware of the circumstances in the game. If there is a good time to look for a runner to tip his intentions, it's when the circumstances say that he ***should*** be stealing. Perhaps the best way to understand the baserunner's intentions is to read a chapter of a book that deals with base stealing. It will help your son understand the runner, if he knows what keys he's looking for in your son's delivery.

After a while your son can develop the instincts for when a runner wants to go. This will help him to use one of these techniques to slow him down.

PICK-OFF MOVES
Generally

Although the purpose of these throws is just to slow down the running game, two general principles will apply if a runner is actually going to be caught. Right-handers will get the runner with the quickness of his move, while lefties will get him with trickery.

Right-handers: First Base Runner

Have your son set up in *the stretch* position, with his hands together. He should bend his knees just slightly so that he is balanced and able to quicken his spin to first base.

Everyone knows that a pitcher will have two moves to first. His slow move, supposedly for the purpose of lulling the runner into a sense of misplaced confidence so that he'll be fooled by the quick move. The problem is that since everyone, especially the base runner, knows that this is the pitcher's slow move, he's not fooled. He's still alert and looking for that fast spin and throw. So have your son show him his quick move. But your son shouldn't show the baserunner his *quickest* move until he's actually trying to catch the runner.

The slow move can be a step off with the right foot; simultaneously the hands separate to the palm away position and then your son steps with his stride foot to first base, and throws hard. Alternatively, he can jump-spin to first by pulling the left shoulder around to his target. The feet will jump only slightly and spin laterally (not backwards or a balk may be called). The feet should just clear the ground by an inch or two. As he jump spins, he must open his hands in an arc to the fully loaded position with the palm away. Now throw hard to first.

Your son should always throw hard, if only to use this as practice for when he's making his best moves. Many young players just lob the ball over on their slow move and then fire the ball into the visitor's dugout when making their quick one. Always be alert for the opportunity to practice a skill, even during a game.

The quicker move is also a jump spin. The difference between this and the slow move is *the feet.* The opening arm arc stays the same in both moves, with the ball taken to *second base.* The spin should be quicker and as low to the ground as possible. Both a slow jump spin and the faster one will have to be practiced in order to get them right. This delivery should be fast enough to make the baserunner think that this is your son's best move. So he should make it look good.

The difference between the quick and *the quickest* jump spin move is in the arm opening. Now have your son shorten his hands separation and take the ball only up to his ear, much like that of how a catcher does when he attempts to throw out the runner. Instead of a short sweeping arc to second base, the hand should be taken up almost on a straight line to just behind the ear. The ball should be pointing off to home plate. This partial ball turn will still permit some extra wrist snap to be added to the throw. Now your son should make his hardest throw to his target, usually the right knee area of a left-handed first baseman.

If he doesn't nail him, remind him that he's only trying to slow him down. This move can be unnerving and will often cause runners to hesitate, so he's done his job.

Throws to First vs. Second and Third

Remember that the big difference between making a move to first base as opposed to second and third is the necessity of actually having to complete the throw. A pitcher can fake a throw to second or third, without having to complete it. But this doesn't mean that if your son starts his motion to first base, he must make the throw.

During the 2006 season, the Toronto Blue Jays' pitcher A.J. Burnett was on the mound with a New York Yankee baserunner at first. Burnett started a throw to first, but noticed that the Jays' first baseman Kyle Overbay was almost fifteen feet off of the bag, looking forward to fielding a hit ball and starting the double play. So Burnett held on to the ball and was called for a balk. But this was the right play to make under those circumstances. Had he thrown to where he thought Overbay would be, the runner would have ended up at third base and the ball down the right field line. As it was, he was limited to just second. So encourage your son to think about the ***possibilities*** that may occur. He'll be a better player for it.

Throws to Second Base

Strangely, most young pitchers seem to focus all of their efforts on holding the baserunner at first base. They step off, vary their tempo, attempt throws and mix it all up, just to ensure that he doesn't steal second. But when he gets to second and he's now in scoring position, he's all but forgotten by most pitchers. This is a mistake. Particularly because now he's more of a threat to score than when he was standing at first base.

THE CLOCKWISE TURN

There are three basic moves to second base. The first is the slower of the two. It requires your son to rotate on his right leg clockwise to second. Your son should pull his stride foot directly back and simultaneously rotate his shoulders in a clockwise fashion. As he does this he must separate his hands to the *palm away* position, ready to throw when the left foot lands. Whether he throws or not is up to him. Sometimes the runner is back in time and other times the fielder won't get back in time. This is a particularly slow move and often does not catch the runner. But for some reason, perhaps it's curious technique, runners hesitate and are occasionally caught.

Some pitchers choose to lift their stride leg up, pause at the top of the lift, and then turn clockwise to go after the runner. The hands separate to the *palm away* position when the pitcher starts his actual turn to second. They feel that this pause will freeze the runner. Your son should experiment to find which technique works best for him.

Step Off and Throw

Like first base, a pitcher can remove his posting foot back behind the rubber and then turn counter-clockwise and throw. This too is a slow motion and is seldom intended to catch a runner. If used in conjunction with the clockwise turn, it has now given the runner two different looks. And it may have just set the runner up to be caught by your son's best move.

The Jump Spin

Once again, the jump spin move is the most effective technique to use when going after the baserunner at second. When he begins his jump, your son must keep his feet low to the ground in order to quicken the spin. The throw should be to the base, not at the fielder moving to it. Aim for a foot or two over the bag. This will require confidence in the fielder to get to the base on time and accuracy in the throw. If both of these elements are not present, don't throw the ball.

Daylight Play

All pick-off moves must be practiced. If your son's team doesn't work at these drills, then he should probably just feint throws to second base.

One of the most common plays to second is the *daylight play*. This is a play which keys on your pitcher seeing daylight between the runner and the shortstop, who must be closer to the base than the runner. When this occurs, the pitcher jump spins and throws to the base. Again two or three feet just above it. It's the shortstop's job to get to the bag.

Often the pitcher will get help on this play from his catcher. A pre-arranged signal, such as the catcher placing his glove face down over the plate, tells the pitcher that the catcher sees the *daylight*, so your son can wheel and throw without even having to first check the baserunner.

But this is a pre-arranged play which must be practiced by all three players. If the shortstop isn't looking in and sees that the glove is face down, he may drift back to this normal fielding position. Often the pitcher will throw through the bag because he *knows* from the catcher's signal that the shortstop is going to be in position to catch his throw. Seldom can a pitcher pull back the throw. Besides, it's a good way for him to injure himself if he tries to hold on to the ball. So practicing pick-off plays is crucial for their success.

TIMING PLAY

Another way of catching the runner at second base is by use of *timing play*. If a pitcher or infielder sees that the runner is taking an unusually large lead, he can flash a signal to run the timing play. It is most often geared to a count of 1000 – 2000 – 3000.

Once either the pitcher or middle infielder has signaled the play, the pitcher will turn his head back to the batter at home plate and count 1000. On a count of 2000 he will pivot to throw to second base just as the infielder is breaking to the bag. On 3000 the ball should be released to second base. Again, at second base the target should be about knee to thigh high, and over the bag.

The advantage of the timing play over the *day light play* is that the middle infielder will not be moving early, so the runner won't be tipped off that a play is on. This should make him an easier target. However in order for this play to work a few things have to happen.

First, either the pitcher or infielder must make a pre-arranged signal in order to alert the other that the play is on. This may be a sweep of a glove down the leg, picking at the shirt or rubbing the ball on the uniform. Second, and most importantly, there must also be a *return signal.* The other player must acknowledge that he has recognized that the play *is on* and return this recognition with an *acknowledgement signal* of his own. If no acknowledgement signal is given, then the play is off. Otherwise a ball could be thrown into center field if the infielder is unaware of the play and his responsibilities.

And lastly, like the *daylight play,* this timing play must be *practiced* if it is to work. You can provide a target standing over second base with a glove held near the knees for your son to practice throwing technique. But if the team doesn't actually practice this play, especially the timing, then your son should just limit himself to step offs and feinting a throw to second. Bill Lee makes this point nicely, "Time plays can go awry if you and your infielders aren't synchronized. That was always a problem for me. My infielders were usually on Greenwich time and I was on Somalian time."

Third Base

Third base is unique. Because the runner is so close to scoring a run, any mistake while trying to catch him off the base is huge. Most pitchers seldom practice this throw, so accuracy is often doubtful. But even if it's an accurate throw, the third baseman has to make a good catch – even if he doesn't make the tag. A mistake by either player, and the run scores. Often the threat of a mistake overwhelmingly outweighs the little chance of catching the runner.

Perhaps even more importantly, pick-off throws shouldn't be made because neither of the reasons for holding a runner close to the base will apply at third base. The runner presents no threat of taking an extra base on a hit, nor will he be prevented from scoring an extra base hit. And these are the original reasons for trying to hold the baserunner to the bag. So don't try to pick off the runner at third base.

Instead, if the baserunner is cheating a good distance down the line, often just staying set and staring at him, or a simple step off, will send him back to the bag.

The Full Windup

Some pitchers go to the full wind-up with a runner at third or if the bases are loaded. The wind-up delivery usually gives the pitcher a couple of miles per hour on his pitch and this makes him feel more comfortable. But many baserunners cheat further down the line believing that a pitcher will never be able to pick them off out of this delivery, without balking. This is a mistake.

If your son decides that he wants to go after such a runner, he must step off the rubber with his posting foot (right) first. If he disengages the rubber with his right foot first he can change the runner or make a throw. But even in this instance, just chasing the runner back to the bag is still the safest play to make.

The Lefthander

As mentioned earlier in these materials dealing with the balk, southpaws have created a different set of rules for the balk and the pick-off move to first base. Because they are facing the runner at first, their move to that base does not rely so much on quickness as it does on a simple deception, even though the balk rule is intended to eliminate any deception by the pitcher.

The Balk Line

A lefthander delivery is controlled by an imaginary line which runs from the pitcher's plate to a spot on the first base line midway between home plate and first. When the pitcher, during his delivery, brings his right leg back to begin his motion to home, he may step to first base if the foot or knee has not been drawn back past this line at the rubber. So long as the pitcher's foot remains on the side of the line closest to home plate, he may step to first base and throw. But if the knee or foot drops back behind this line, the pitcher is committed to go home with the ball. If he steps to first, it's a balk.

Watch the Runner

Because he is facing the runner, he starts off by staring at the runner while he is in the set position, after having taken the pitch signal from his catcher. Then as he starts his delivery, his eyes should shift slightly down the line but not immediately to his target. By keeping the eyes focused just down the line, he appears to still be looking at the baserunner. This deception should hold the runner at the base longer. Then as the stride foot passes the imaginary line to the first base line, your son should shift his focus to his target at home plate. This technique will take a stride or two away from the runner. Because many lefties use this technique, sometimes not watching the runner can be equally effective. Rather than stare at the runner to start the delivery, instead have your son look to home plate. Then as he starts to bring his stride foot back have him look directly at the runner. This will often cause the runner to freeze, not knowing whether your son will go after him or to the plate. Then throw home.

Some pitchers will try to bring their stride leg back behind the imaginary line and still try to go after the runner. A lefty's front foot will often be taken behind the balk line while being pointed towards the second base area. So often, a pitcher will try to keep the front foot pointed towards first base in order to give the impression that the foot hasn't dropped back behind the balk line. Sometimes this works.

What Kind of Action?

When going after the runner, your son can use either a shortened throw from the ear or sidearm motion to the bag. It will be up to your son and how comfortable, as well as effective, he feels making these throws. The overhand throw tends to have more velocity and greater accuracy. But the throw is very obvious and clearly gives away the play earlier. The sidearm throw is more deceptive and can be delivered from the set position with a less obvious motion. However, if your son is off the target at all with this throw it will be wide left or right. Usually the runner ends up at second base. On the other hand, a throw from the ear usually ends up low or high of the target when it isn't executed properly. Often these balls can still be caught or at least knocked down. The runner is usually still at first base when the ball is thrown back to the pitcher.

In either instance it will help convince the umpire that your son has not broken the balk line with his foot if he steps to first as he makes his throw. Many pitchers find the sidearm throw the more fluid of the two throws if they are going to use this ***step and throw*** technique.

Borrow From the Right-hander

The lefthander should borrow some of the baserunner *controlling techniques* used by right-handers. Your son should step off, vary his throws over, change his pitching cadence, quick pitch and so on, just like the right-hander. Remember the name of the game is to keep the runner off balance and upset his timing. If your son can do this with all of these tools then he's done his job. But remind him that his first priority is always the batter.

Understand the 3-D Strike-Zone

Earlier in this book we looked at the size of the strike zone and learned that it is significantly wider than the actual 17-inch plate. But there is another dimension to the ***k-zone*** that has yet to be explained: its depth.

The depth of the plate is 17 inches and your son should use all of it. A strike occurs when any part of the ball passes over any part of the plate. This is important for anyone who throws pitches that *break* sideways. If your son throws a cutter, sinker or curveball, the pitch may not be in the strike zone when the ball reaches the front edge of the plate. But this pitch may *break* into the strike zone as it passes over the back part of the plate. Your son must eventually improve his pitch location to the point that his breaking balls in particular will pass over the rear position of the plate for a strike.

When your son throws his curveball off the plate inside, which then breaks over the plate for a strike, this pitch is called a *back-up pitch*, because it often causes the batter to do exactly that. When he throws this same pitch to a left handed batter for a strike, it's referred to as a *backdoor pitch*. In both instances, he's using his knowledge of the depth of the plate to make his breaking pitches even more effective.

What About Strike Zone Height?

The rules say that the strike zone extends from the bottom of the knee cap to the half-way point between the batter's waist and shoulders. This is generally accepted as the chest or at *the letters*. Thus the strike zone varies from one batter to another.

On August 1951, Bill Veek, owner of the St. Louis Browns, had Eddie Gaedel penciled into his team's leadoff spot. Eddie stood only three feet seven inches tall. This presented little more than eight to ten inches of strike zone for the pitcher to hit. Needless to say, Eddie Gaedel was walked and immediately replaced for a pinch runner, never to suit up again. Bill Veek's playful gesture illustrates that the range of the strike zone size varies from batter to batter.

What if the Batter Crouches?

Many batters sit down in a crouch to hit. Pete Rose was well known for this kind of stance and more recently David Eckstein employs a crouch. But does this ***shrink*** the strike zone? If so, how do you pitch to this kind of batter?

Your son shouldn't worry about a shrinking strike zone when pitching to *crouchers*. Actually your son often has an advantage with these types of hitters. The rules of baseball state: "The strike zone shall be determined from the batter's stance as the batter prepares to swing at a pitch." Importantly, the underlined part has been interpreted as occurring just as the batter starts his swing. Thus when a batter starts out in a crouch but then straightens up to take his swing, his high end of the strike zone is determined at this point. Since all players who start in a crouch always straighten up to some extent when swinging at the ball, their strike zone actually grows in size. And this is where a pitcher can have an advantage with batters who crouch.

If a batter straightens up four or five inches out of his crouch in order to swing, he's vulnerable for a pitch thrown at this shoulder height. Usually he won't swing at this pitch because it's too high. But it isn't! It becomes a strike when he straightens up to swing. Crouching batters are notorious low-ball hitters because this is usually all pitchers think about throwing to them due to their stance. They don't adjust well to pitches thrown high in their strike zone. And are often *caught looking* at strikes thrown at their shoulder because they usually don't adjust to the new perspective created by their batting stance.

The Balk

The Balk rule is perhaps both the most confusing rule in baseball and the most misunderstood. It is the most confusing because the rule itself sets out only some of the specific forms of violation, while leaving it up to the umpire to interpret and enforce other variations of the rule. The result is that the balk rule will change with the delivery style of every pitcher and every umpire's own judgment on the play.

Much of the confusion regarding the balk rule would be simplified if the pitcher knows why the rule was created and what it is trying to accomplish.

THE RULE

The balk rule is found in section 8.05 of The Official Rules of Major League Baseball. This rule states:

> 8.05 If there is a runner, or runners, it is a balk when –
>
> (a) The pitcher, while touching his plate, makes any motion naturally associated with his pitch and fails to make such a delivery;
>
> (b) The pitcher, while touching his plate, feints a throw to first base and fails to complete the throw;
>
> (c) The pitcher, while touching his plate, fails to step directly toward a base before throwing to that base;
>
> (d) The pitcher, while touching his plate, throws, or feints a throw to an unoccupied base, except for the purpose of making a play;
>
> (e) The pitcher makes an illegal pitch;
>
> (f) The pitcher delivers the ball to the batter while he is not facing the batter;
>
> (g) The pitcher makes any motion naturally associated with his pitch while he is not touching the pitcher's plate;
>
> (h) The pitcher unnecessarily delays the game;
>
> (i) The pitcher, without having the ball, stands on or astride the pitcher's plate or while off the plate, he feints a pitch;
>
> (j) The pitcher, after coming to a legal pitching position, removes one hand from the ball other than in an actual pitch, or throwing to a base;

(k) The pitcher, while touching his plate, accidentally or intentionally drops the ball;
(l) The pitcher, while giving an intentional base on balls, pitches when the catcher is not in the catcher's box;
(m) The pitcher delivers the pitch from Set Position without coming to a stop.

The penalty for committing a balk is to award one base for any and all runners on the base paths. In some circumstances, such as for violations of subsection (e) and (h), the batter may also be awarded a called ***ball***.

Guiding Principle to the Rule

An annotated copy of the rules of baseball provides a number of examples as to how certain subsections should be applied. Importantly, it also clarifies the purpose of this rule. It states: "Umpires should bear in mind that the purpose of the balk rule is to prevent the pitcher from *deliberately deceiving* the base runner".

Historically

The balk rule was established in 1845 in the Knickerbocker Rules, although in a different form than today's version. Prior to the creation of this rule, a pitcher would typically stop halfway through his delivery, wheel, and then throw out a runner trying to steal a base. With any practice at all of this move, most runners were easily caught and eliminated from the base paths. But as a result, games were very low scoring. This was also long before the home run became a popular way of bringing home baserunners. Until "the Babe" established the home run in the 1920's as a serious offensive weapon, hitters just focused on putting the ball in play. They hoped that the ball found a hole or that an error occurred, on either the throw or the catch. But when they did get on base and then were eliminated with the pitcher's deceptive delivery, the result was a low scoring game. So the balk rule was instituted to make the game more exciting on the base paths and bring more scoring to home plate. The fans responded enthusiastically to this increased offense in the game.

Knowing *what* the balk rule is intended to accomplish and that the pitcher is not permitted to *deliberately deceive* the runner helps us to understand how the rule will be enforced. The following list provides just some of the ways this rule has been interpreted.

Balk Clarifications and Explanations

Subsection (a)

A pitcher who makes any motion *naturally associated* with his pitching delivery but does not throw home commits a balk. Many years ago David Wells, while pitching for the Yankees, pumped his hands over his head to begin his delivery and accidentally knocked his cap off. So he stopped and bent over to pick it up. Balk! He had started his delivery but did not complete the pitch.

But not just any pitching motion will be considered the start of your son's delivery. For example, if while in the stretch, he separates his hands and then steps directly to first base and throws over, this is a legal *pick-off move*.

On the other hand, if during this pick-off attempt, he first brought his stride foot directly back on a line between home plate and the pitching rubber, this is a balk. Even if he steps to first base and throws. This small straight back motion of his foot will be viewed as part of his normal delivery and an *attempt to deceive* the runner.

A legal step to first base will not include any foot motion backwards, but simply a lateral swing of the foot towards first base.

Subsection (b)

If a pitcher feints a throw to first base but does not make the throw, this is a balk. Many balks are called because of this rule, but not because the pitcher steps to first base and only pretends to throw over. The rule is interpreted much more subtly.

Your son is permitted to turn his head to first base to check the runner. But he is not permitted to also turn his left shoulder in that direction, even slightly, or he will be called for a balk. This limited shoulder motion will be viewed as *a movement* to first base but without a throw over. So it is seen as a *feint* move. Similarly, if your son moves his hands up and down or accidentally flexes his stride or posting leg knee, then these very small motions will also be seen as movements to first, or a *deception*, to fool the runner. Balk!

So if your son is on the rubber and he wants to scratch an itch or adjust his uniform, remind him to *step off* first. Whenever in doubt, step off!

<u>Subsection (c)</u>

If a pitcher is going to throw to first base or throw, or feint a throw, to second or third base, he must first step to the base *before* he releases the ball. Without a rule like this, pitchers would simply sling or flip a ball to the base, giving the runner little chance to move up. Again remember that the balk rule is intended to encourage excitement and offense on the field.

Importantly, if your son is stepping to second or third base, unlike first base, he does not have to actually throw the ball to these bases. But he still must make a definitive step.

In spite of this requirement that the pitcher must make a definitive step before he throws to a base, the *jump spin* move is both legal and the most effective pick-off move for a right-hander. It will be described in the following section.

Subsection (d)

Unless the pitcher is making an actual play, he may not throw or fake a throw to an unoccupied base. Such a motion is viewed as trying to induce the runner at another base (usually third) to try to steal home. And this is viewed as deception.

Subsection (e)

Making any *illegal pitch* will result in a balk. The most common illegal pitch thrown, when runners are on base, is the *quick pitch*. Sometimes a pitcher will quickly release the ball to home in order to surprise the runner. However, if the batter is not given a reasonable amount of time to set up, the umpire will call an illegal pitch and a balk.

The legal way to quicken a pitcher's movement to home and thereby give the runner less time to get a jump on the play is by shortening his leg lift. This is commonly referred to as a *slide step* delivery. By eliminating the high knee lift, the pitcher can get the ball into the catcher's glove faster and in doing so discourage the runner from stealing a base.

However, if the slide step delivery is used but before the batter is set up in the box, it too will be viewed as an illegal pitch and a balk will be called.

Subsection (f)

The pitcher must be facing the batter as he releases the pitch or this will be a balk. Once again, the issue is one of deception and the possibility of injuring the hitter, if the pitcher releases the ball without looking towards the batter. Without this rule, a pitcher might try to fool the runner by looking over towards him while releasing the ball to home plate. Such a motion would clearly be intended to deceive the runner and thus offend the balk rule. More importantly, the batter would be prone to being hit by the ball and so, also for safety reasons, such a delivery is prohibited.

Subsection (g)

The pitcher may only make his pitching delivery motion if he is in contact with the rubber. If he makes any of these motions but is not in contact with the pitcher's plate, it is a balk. This rule is clearly intended to protect the runner from deception.

So if a team is going to try to tag the runner out using the *hidden ball* play, then the pitcher must not step onto the mound and pretend to begin his normal delivery. If he does, it's a balk.

Subsection (h)

The pitcher cannot unnecessarily delay the game. Runners can often worry a pitcher so much that he lengthens the time between his pitches. Or, a pitcher may constantly make so many pick-off throws to a base to hold the runner that the game slows to a crawl. In order to keep the game and the action moving, an umpire will first warn the pitcher about this delay of game. Sometimes a second warning will be given. But never a third. Instead, the umpire will call a balk, thereby allowing the runner who the pitcher was trying to hold at the base the opportunity to walk to the next one. The umpire will also award a called *ball* to the batter.

This should never occur. No pitcher should ever become so distracted by a base runner that he allows this to happen. If it does occur, a pitcher has a much bigger problem than just having a runner on the base paths.

Subsection (i)

A pitcher who is not in possession of the ball cannot step onto or stand astride the pitcher's plate. Such an action will be interpreted as a clear intention to *deceive* the runner. This mistake is usually committed when the *hidden ball* play is on and the pitcher forgets this rule.

Subsection (j)

While in the set or wind-up positions, the pitcher may not remove one hand from the ball unless he is separating his hands to throw home or to a base. Without this rule, the runner could be easily deceived and picked off of the base. If the pitcher has set his hands together while on the rubber, he must step off of the pitcher's plate if he intends to separate his hands. Otherwise if he does not go home, throw to a bag, or feint a throw to a base, this will be a balk.

Subsection (k)

If the pitcher drops the ball while in or coming out of the set or wind-up positions, this is a balk. Similarly, if a ball slips out of his hand during his throw but does not cross either the first or third base lines, this too is a balk under this subsection.

Subsection (l)

If, while intentionally pitching out to walk the batter, the catcher steps out of his catcher's box before the ball releases from the pitcher's hand, this is a balk. The catcher must limit his movement. While standing up, he should hold his glove or bare hand out to his side, and then step out to the ball after the ball has left the pitcher's hand.

Subsection (m)

Pitching out of the set position, the pitcher must bring his hands together for a noticeable stop (between his waist and chest) before he delivers the ball to the plate. This failure to come set can also be called as a ***quick pitch*** and as such, also a violation of subsection (e).

Other Balks

When throwing out of the stretch, the pitcher must take the catcher's signals with his hands separated down at his sides.

If a pitcher brings his stride foot back of the rubber, he must deliver the ball to home, unless he is taking his foot back to second base in a pickoff move. He need not throw the ball (subsection (a)).

Many pitchers try to pick off the runner at first base by initially going after the runner on third. Typically a right-hander will turn and step to third base with a feint and then turn 180 degrees, to pick off the runner leading off first base. But sometimes a pitcher will be called for a balk on this move. A pitcher can avoid the balk by taking a definitive step to third and then turning to first for the throw. But if the move is a quick step to third with a seamless spin to first base, this will be viewed as ***deception***. And a balk will be called.

The ***jump spin*** move, used most successfully by right-handers, is a legal pick-off move. But like the third to first move, this move will ***sometimes*** be called a balk. The jump spin move requires that the pitcher spin out of his stretch position to first base and make a quick throw. But if the spin and throw appears to the umpire as one ***seamless*** move, then this violates subsection (c), which requires that the pitcher first step (noticeably) before his throw. So to avoid the balk call, your son must delay his throw just enough so that this looks like two separate actions.

The feint to third base, then wheel and throw to catch the runner at first may be called a balk for another reason. A right-handed pitcher may lift his knee and then step to third base to make a throw. But, if while lifting his stride leg, the knee drops back past the imaginary line that runs directly between the rubber and third base, the pitcher must throw home. Raising the knee past this imaginary line or taking his stride foot back to the rubber will be interpreted as the pitcher beginning his normal pitching motion to the plate. If he makes either of these moves and does not go home, he will violate subsection (a). For a further explanation, see the following heading: Left-Handed Pitchers.

A pitcher cannot come set with his hands more than once. In the movie Major League III, a pitcher on the minor league team set his hands three times before he finally delivered the ball to home. This would constitute a balk. Allowing a pitcher to set his hands and then reset them again would permit a pitcher to fool the runner by sometimes throwing home after the first set, but then adding a ***reset*** to the next delivery. The mixing in of the resetting of hands would force the runner to wait until the pitcher was actually into his stride before the runner made any attempt to the next base. This would virtually eliminate any chance of a running game. (Rule subsection (a)).

The Full Wind Up

With only a runner at third base or if the bases are juiced, some pitchers prefer to pitch out of the full wind up position. But once on the rubber with both feet, how does he step off to get the runner at third base, without committing a balk? Many young players believe that once the pitcher is in the wind-up he can't step off without balking. So the runner will cheat half way down the line. But they are wrong and can be caught off base without a balk being called on the pitcher.

The normal delivery out of the wind-up requires the pitcher to take his *left* foot back behind the pitcher's plate in a *rocker step*. The right foot is then adjusted to lie beside and in contact with the rubber. To avoid a balk your son will have to step back with his *right* foot before making any play on the runner. If he was permitted to step back with his normal rocker step (left) before making a move to third base, then this would require the runner to hold at the base until he could determine whether this was a pitch to home or a pickoff move. This move would therefore constitute a deception. So the pitcher must step off the rubber with his right foot, whether he is attempting a pick-off or just to adjust his cap. If he forgets and steps off with his left foot, then he violates subsection (a).

Left-Handed Pitchers

Major League baseball had to develop special interpretations of the balk rule in order to control lefties. Southpaws have a decided advantage in controlling the runners at first base, because they are facing in that direction when they come set. In fact, without these interpretations, lefties could kill the running game.

So baseball rules developed a theoretical line drawn from the rubber to the baseline halfway between the pitcher's plate and first base. This unseen line approximates an angle of 45 degrees. If a left-hander takes this foot over this line during his delivery, he must continue to take the ball to home. Another way to look at this is that the pitcher must step to the second-base side of this line if he goes to first base. If the foot lands on the home plate side of the 45-degree line but he throws to first base, it is a balk.

Another balk will be called if a lefty brings his stride foot back behind the rubber during his delivery. Even if he then strides to first base on the proper side of the 45-degree line. Both of these balk rule interpretations fall under subsection 8.05(a).

A Catcher's Balk

Sometimes you will hear an umpire call a balk on a *catcher*. What has happened is that the catcher has somehow interfered with the batter's attempt to hit the ball. The catcher need not actually touch the hitter or his bat, so long as it appears that the catcher somehow interfered with the swing. Often this occurs because the catcher has reached too far into the strike zone with his glove.

Some may call this *catcher's interference* but like a balk called on a pitcher, the penalty is to award a base to any runner on the base paths. If the batter does not make contact with the ball, the play is dead. And the batter is awarded a called ball.

Nullified Balks

If a pitcher commits any of the aforementioned violations, he can be called for a balk. However, if the pitcher was induced by anyone from the opposing team to commit the balk, it will be nullified.

Usually a call from the opposing bench for a *timeout* when no player on the field is asking for one will often cause the pitcher to halt his delivery in mid-stride. If one of the umpires has called a balk but then realizes that a bogus timeout call was made, the balk call will be nullified. Often the person who induced the balk with the call for timeout will be ejected from the game.

Frequency of Balk Calls

Although the balk rule has been around for more than a century, the frequency of balk calls has varied over the years. In 1978 the balk was rigorously enforced by Major League Baseball. Again ten years later, during the first eleven days of the 1988 season, 128 balk calls were made, 88 in the American League and 36 in the National League. This resulted in The Sporting News running an article entitled "Balkamania Unchecked," as well as commenting on the umpires' renewed interest in the rule.

But neither the rule itself nor a revolution in pitching deliveries had occurred. Rather, if pitchers are more successful in holding runners and thereby limiting offence, then the offices of Major League Baseball encourage umpires to be more observant of pitchers. Alternatively, if the trend is more to the long ball and less *small ball* base stealing, then again umpires may be encouraged to enforce the balk rule more rigorously.

But your son need not worry about these ebbs and flows for his game. At lower levels of baseball the balk is often enforced less rigorously. Particularly at lower levels of youth ball, where players are just trying to learn the game, umpires are often more flexible in what they will call. In fact, many umpiring associations will instruct their members to caution pitchers regarding their delivery and explain to them what will constitute a balk before they call it. And this is how it should be. The players want to know if they're doing something wrong, and a helpful explanation and even a demonstration will be well received. The game can only improve with this kind of umpiring approach.

Controlling the Runner

Controlling the other team's running game requires knowing your objective. The true speedster who also has base-stealing knowledge and an instinctive feel for running will not be caught. So your son shouldn't put a lot of effort into holding him at first or second. Worse still, don't let the runner distract your son from his primary focus – the batter. If a runner is smart and quick, he's going to swipe the bag. So it's the other runners that your son should focus on.

Your son must never let someone steal a base who doesn't really have the ability to do this. If it happens, something's wrong with your son's approach. It is these other batters whom your lad must control by using techniques such as a step off, varying his delivery, staring at the batter and so on. Just like the *big batter* who irrespectively will get his certain number of big hits, so will the *big time base stealer*. Your son must stop the other average runners. Therefore it becomes very important that your son control the average base stealer. This will also help him to stay out of the *big inning*.

Avoiding the Balk

Your son can avoid a called balk by adhering to the following:

1. Find a place on the rubber where he can see first base with only a turn of his head.
2. Stand on the rubber with the side of his right foot touching the pitcher's plate and his left foot about shoulder-width directly to home plate. If the front (left) foot is not directly in front of the right but is a few more inches closer to the third base line, then he won't be able to see first base with just the head turn alone.
3. Take the catcher's signals standing with his foot on the rubber and his hands down at his sides.
4. Come set with the hands somewhere between the waist and chest. If needed, re-set the stride foot to a comfortable distance for the delivery home or for a throw to a base. But reset the feet before he brings his hands together.
5. Check the runners by moving only the head, leaving the shoulders, arms and legs where they are.
6. Deliver the ball to home or make a move to an occupied base, leading with a definitive step in that direction.
7. Re-set and repeat.

FIELDING IN THE PITCHER'S POSITION

Every time a ball is hit, the pitcher must be ready to help out. Sometimes the ball will be hit back towards the mound, a bunt may be placed in front of the pitcher or a ball is hit safely with a runner already on base. In all of these instances your son must be ready to react, either make or help out on the play.

There are too many situations which a pitcher must react to in order to back up a play to be mentioned here. I recommend Coach Ron Polk's book, *Baseball Playbook*, for an excellent review of pitcher responsibilities on a hit ball. However, a few situations that are the most common for all pitchers will be outlined briefly.

Move Somewhere

Any time a ball is hit, your son should move somewhere. It's a mistake to just stand still and watch the play. Usually fly balls and one-hop ground balls are caught. But what if they're not? Now the batter is off and running, and a pitcher who is still standing on the mound can't be any part of a play to stop him. Even if this only means moving towards first or second base, to back up the play on an error, move somewhere!

Leo Mazzone's recommendations are the best place for your son to start learning this aspect of the game.

Runner on first, base hit	*you back up third base*
Runner on second, base hit	*you back up home plate*
Two runners on, base hit	*you follow the ball and back up wherever the ball is heading*

You follow the ball; the goal is to be in the right place at the right time to handle an errant overthrow of a base.

And one might add one other direction for your son to work at: on any ball hit to the right field side of the diamond, your son should run to cover first base, since the first baseman may be pulled off the bag and need someone to receive his throw on the ball he fielded.

Infield Pop-Up

A recent habit has crept into baseball, at all levels, and it's a mistake. On a pop up in the infield, pitchers are often seen pointing at the ball in the air. For some reason they think that this is helpful. The only time that this can be of any use to anyone is if the ball is hit back of the catcher into foul territory, and only if the catcher has lost the ball because it has gone behind him. Only in this instance will standing on the mound and pointing at the ball in the air be an useful exercise.

But this isn't the only time this pointing business creeps into the pitcher's habits. Pitchers often stand pointing at the ball hit just behind the mound, to one side or another. It's nearly impossible for the middle infielders not to see this ball, so why is the pitcher still pointing at it? Particularly if he could be moving to back up any base, just in case the ball is dropped and the runners are moving.

Worse still, most pitchers don't actually point at the ball's location in the air. Instead the pitcher points directly over his head while simultaneously looking at the ground. Perhaps he's tracking its shadow. But if the ball was hit directly above this pitcher and no infielder made a play on it, the only way he would know it wasn't going to be caught is when the ball hit directly on the top of his head. So instead of pointing up, make sure your son is moving somewhere to help out.

Fielding Pop-Ups

A ball popped up behind the mound is the responsibility of middle infielders. A ball hit between the mound and home plate, as well as just off to the sides of the plate, should be left for the catcher. But a ball popped back to the mound and often directly towards either base line falls within the range of the pitcher. Unless the catcher has called for the ball, your son should go after it.

If the pitcher and catcher call for the ball, whether in the air or on the ground (i.e. bunt) the pitcher must always back off the ball. The catcher has priority. So if the ball has been popped up, your son must avoid running into the catcher who is trying to track it down. The catcher won't be looking out for the pitcher, so your son must look out for him.

When he hears the catcher's call, his first action must be to locate the catcher, not the ball. He should then keep his eyes on the catcher and peel away from whatever direction the catcher is moving. If he were to watch the ball and not his catcher, the odds are that they would run in to one another and the ball would be dropped.

Your son can also help out his catcher by reassuring him that the catch is his to make, and not your son's. This *communication* can be key to avoiding a situation where both the pitcher and catcher back away from the ball because each has heard the other call for it.

Your son should just call *yours* or you, whichever term that has been approved by the coach, for situations where two fielders have made a call for the ball. This will reassure the catcher that the play is his to make, and he can do so with aggressiveness.

Use a Two-Handed Catch

A ball popped up in the infield often has as much energy in the ball as one hit into the outfield. But the energy of an infield popup expresses itself as ***spin***, not distance. This means that, unless your son uses both hands to catch and close down the glove on the ball, it will end up spinning out of his glove if he tries to make a *one-handed* catch. He should use *two hands*, just to be sure.

Ground Ball Come-Backers

Often the ball will be hit directly back to your son while he is still positioned on the mound. In reaction to a *come backer* he has to focus on doing two things. First, after looking the ball into the glove he will usually have to be *patient* while the first baseman gets to, and sets up at, his base. Your son shouldn't have to rush the throw since the batter won't beat the ball to the bag, so don't lead the first baseman with the throw. Wait for him to set up first and then make a solid, accurate throw.

Second, because your son is standing on an uneven surface (the mound) he should pay attention to his footwork. As the first baseman reaches the bag, your son should execute a shuffle step or step-over technique that will take his momentum to first. This should make it easier to throw the ball than having to *muscle* it there from a dead stop and perhaps making an inaccurate throw in the process. Remind him to fix his eyes directly on the chest or glove of the first baseman, whichever is inside the baseline.

Slow Rollers and Bunts

Both slow-rolling hits and bunted balls must be approached quickly, but all the while the body must be in control. The way to do this is to have your son first take long or normal running strides in pursuit of the ball, but then shorten them into choppy steps as he approaches it. This will permit him to maximize his balance when picking up the ball and making the throw.

As he gets to the ball, he should try to scoop the ball with the glove into the hand. This will permit him to continue this left to right motion, while bringing the ball up with both hands to just behind his head. He's now ready to step and release the ball to first base. If he had taken the ball with his bare hand into his glove, a right to left motion, he would have to first reverse the direction of his arm movement in order to get the ball into a *loaded* position. This will take too long, if the runner has any speed.

If the ball is dead when he gets to it, he should land his feet such that the ball is just in front of this rear (right) foot and the left foot is directly on a line to his target. The only time your son should field the ball with his bare hand is if it has stopped rolling. Initially he should grasp the ball by pressing it into the ground as he secures his grip. Later, as he becomes more comfortable fielding, he can scoop the ball up barehanded with both of his throwing fingers under the ball, ready to throw.

Throws to Second Base

A ball hit directly back to your son on the mound will require him to pivot and throw to second. This won't be a long toss so he won't have to step or shuffle to the base as he throws. His turning to throw should give him enough body momentum.

With a runner at first, any ground ball in the infield will have one of the middle infielders moving to second base in order to start the double play. But if the ball is hit sharply to your son, when he pivots to throw, the infielder may not yet be at the base. So he must time his throw so as to allow the fielder to reach the bag before the ball arrives.

Have him make a slight shuffle of his feet as he throws, in order to avoid being tense while throwing flatfooted. The target should be about chest high and just over the bag.

Throws to Third Base

Seldom should your son be making a throw to third base to get the runner. The play to third base on a ball hit ***slowly*** to a right-handed pitcher is virtually impossible for young players to make. Your son's momentum from his delivery will be taking him towards the first base line. Fielding this ball quickly enough to turn and then step to third base with the throw can only be made by an older, stronger and more experienced player.

For such a player, a number of things must happen. First, he should only attempt this throw if he hears his catcher calling for it. Usually "three" is the signal. Because this squeeze play is difficult to turn, the catcher will only be calling for it if it is an important play (i.e. late and the game is tied).

If the ball is *hit sharply* to the pitcher's bare-hand side, it's doubtful that he will be able to knock it down to make the play. Instead, he should leave this ball for his shortstop. But a ball hit hard to his glove side may be caught. He should then turn and take a step to third with the target chest-high over the bag.

When a bunted ball or slow roller takes your son to the third base side, he may be able to field this ball if he has very quick feet. Often the only throw will be an underhand toss to the bag. Perhaps a little *push throw* with the ball held high may get the runner. But often, only a quick catcher will have time to make this play in time. Remember that the runner will have a lead off and probably only need to cover seventy-eight feet or so, at contact. In this case it is smarter to go after the batter at first base to get at least one out.

Stay Out of the Big Inning

All fielders, including the pitcher, should always keep in mind that a principle goal is to stay out of the big inning. This means quite simply, "Be sure you get an out."

Trying to turn the double play to get out of the inning is commendable. But only if it works. Your son has to recognize the quality of players on his team and play to that level. If he might be late to the base with the ball, may have to make a difficult throw or his infielder has wooden hands, don't throw the ball. Instead, turn and get the batter going to first, because if the play at second isn't made then the runner at first is usually safe. Now with none out, this can often lead to a big inning. And big innings are pitcher killers. Sometimes the game is already over after the fourth inning.

Communication

Communication is key to a pitcher successfully fielding his position. Whether it is the key to avoiding the pitcher and catcher colliding while both making a play on the ball, or listening for the catcher's command for where your son should throw the ball, communication is vital to good baseball.

Usually the catcher will be calling the play or the third baseman will be calling off both your son and the catcher so he can make the catch. But your son can have a role to play by supporting other players by yelling for the ball to be thrown to "one" or "two." He can also assist by yelling "you" or "yours," as explained earlier to help reassure a player that the ball is his to field. Whenever possible, your son should try to find a way to help a play be successfully executed through loud and clear communication.

Fielding Drills

Drill #1

Place a number of balls around and in front of the mound to simulate where a bunt or weakly-hit grounder will come to rest. Your son should mimic his delivery but without using the arms. Now field one of the balls and throw to first base. Repeat this drill until all of the balls have been fielded and thrown.

Drill #2

Repeat Drill #1 but now throw to second, third and home plate. The throw to home will usually be underhand. However when fielding a ball down the first base line he will pick up the ball, pivot and then throw home. Throw the ball with a little something on it at knee height but don't drill it through the catcher.

Drill #3

Roll or softly hit some balls towards and beside the mound. Your son should be reacting to these balls out of the position he ends up in at the end of his delivery. Now throw the ball to first, second, third and home.

Drill #4

Repeat drill #3, but this time hit some harder comebackers to your son.

Drill #5

Either throw or hit some pop flies into the shallow area of the infield where your son would normally be responsible for the catch. As he's moving to the ball have him yell out "mine" or "I've got it" to mimic a game situation. If he doesn't practice this, he won't do it in a game.

Since the accuracy of these pop flies is vital, you may wish to use a tennis racquet to ensure the ball goes where you want it to.

RECOMMENDED READING

Baseball Playbook, Ron Polk

Baseball Field Guide, Dan Formosa and Paul Hamburger

The Complete Book of Pitching, Doug Myers and Mark Gola

The Complete Book of Baseball Signs and Plays, Stu Southworth

Pitch Like a Pro, Leo Mazzone

CHAPTER 4
UNDERSTANDING THE BATTER

This Chapter

Few young pitchers go to the mound intent upon using any particular pitching strategy. The prior chapters have given your son the tools with which he can apply several pitching strategies. However, although he may know what it is that he wants to do, it may also be useful for him to know what the batter wants to do and what the hitter is not capable of doing.

This chapter is designed to describe what strategy many batters are intending to use against your son, as well as describing hitting weaknesses that they may have but know nothing about. Your son can use this information against all of the batters which he will face.

Sitting on the Fastball

Most batters, especially the young ones, *sit on the fastball* or *sit red.* This simply means that the batter is all set to swing hard from his heels and hit the next fastball out of the park.

I once saw a local little league team that dominated its opponents by out swinging them and often jacking pitches over the fence. Here was an entire team which *sat red,* often on the pitcher's very first pitch. These kids were actually competing with one another for who could launch the most round-trippers. Many coaches approached this team with trepidation. Your son should approach such a situation with a sense of opportunity.

I suggested to the coach of the team next scheduled to play this free swinging club that he might want to try pitching them soft to hard. Apparently heeding my advice, his pitcher went out and threw more soft-breaking pitches like a change-up, curve and even a lower end fastball, and then would come back with a hard fastball. Especially hard and high. These batters were confused by the soft pitches both in and out of the strike zone. But because of their own aggressive natures they just couldn't help themselves, so they swung at all the pitches thrown. Then when the pitcher threw his fastball behind a change-up, the pitch looked twice as fast. Because the slower breaking pitches had also upset the hitter's timing, the batter simply couldn't catch up to the fastball. This team of power hitters that everyone had feared was shut off of the scoreboard in this game. Whether it's a power hitting player or an entire team of power hitters, your son will always be able to find the Achilles heel of his opponents.

In instances such as this, pitching *soft to hard* is often the answer. Perhaps start with a fastball away, maybe even off of the plate. Then he should throw mostly breaking pitches which have movement and will slow down the batter's timing. Now the hitter's susceptible to a fastball, particularly one on the inside of the plate. But don't be predictable by always throwing the same sequence. Your son should constantly mix up his pitches to keep the batters off balance.

The Batter's Strike Zone

Most young batters do not understand the dimension of the width of the strike zone and this makes them vulnerable. Three major league rules describe the width of the strike zone very clearly. The first lesson for a pitcher is to understand that it takes the combination of three rules or principles to describe the strike zone. This was described in an earlier chapter but is worth repeating *vis* the batter's perspective.

First, we start with a plate 17 inches in width. Second, the rules tell us that any pitch thrown anywhere over the plate is a strike. And third, all major league balls must be no wider than 2 inches to 2 ½ inches in diameter. Now we begin throwing at a 17-inch wide plate. But when only a quarter-inch of the ball passes over the outside corner of the plate, this too is a strike. Since rule two says any portion of the ball over any portion of the plate is a strike, this means that the plate on the outside corner is now 2 inches wider, or 21 inches in width. Then if you also add the same thinking to the inside corner, when the outside of the ball just kisses the corner, the full width of the strike zone is now at least 21 inches. But there's more.

The Major League umpires are permitted to add a single ball width to both the inside and outside corners of the plate. This now brings the strike zone to 25 inches in width. The umpires seldom call this entire strike zone but the point to be understood is that the major league strike zone is considerably larger than 17 inches in width. In most jurisdictions which are non-professional (i.e. youth leagues) umpires are encouraged only to add a pitch on the outside. Still this gives a pitcher not a 17-inch target to hit but one closer to 23 inches. This explanation often elicits a broad smile from the pitcher.

But your son has yet another advantage in knowing the actual dimensions of the strike zone, because most batters are simply unaware of these broad dimensions. Most hitters believe that the 17-inch plate face is all that determines the strike zone. So the batter watches pitches both away and inside, which he thinks are balls but are called for strikes. This batter simply has not been properly taught to manage the strike zone in its proper dimensions. But if a batter is going to dominate the strike zone, first he must understand it. This is where too many coaches let their players down. Your son can exploit this misunderstanding to his advantage simply by pitching in and out to the corners.

Dominant Hand Theory Again

The following strategies can be applied to a batter whom your son has never seen before or knows nothing about his tendencies. But it can also be effectively used against hitters that your son has already faced as well. As you will see, this theory has a broad application.

Dominant Hand Theory applies to our everyday lives as well as all sports. In general, it simply means that all people have a tendency to be physically biased on one side of the body, whether they're a lefty or right-handed. Approximately ten percent of the population has more refined motor skills on the left side of the body. In turn this bias will have an effect upon how we walk, run, throw, write and even how we see things. Naturally, it also has an implication for how a batter swings a bat. In particular, statistical analysis has demonstrated that right-handed batters hit certain pitches well and certain other pitches, not so well. Similarly, the same statistical work tells us that left-handed hitters also have certain hitting areas of both strength and weakness, although quite different from the righty. Since Jeremy always found it easier to remember these areas by starting with a left-handed hitter, that's how we'll begin.

Statistics show us that a normal left-handed hitter will be strong when swinging at the pitch low and inside (actually middle of the plate and in). To at least some extent this will be as a result of right-handed pitchers so often throwing down and away to the right handed hitters (who are the majority of batters). Consequently, the pitcher throws mostly towards the left hand side of the plate. Changing this tendency is difficult for many pitchers, particularly the young ones. So the left-handed batter simply sees a lot of pitches thrown to him inside. It's no wonder that he gets used to hitting these pitches, since he sees so many of them.

The second area of strength for the lefty is the high pitch on the outside corner of the plate. In a moment I'll explain why this is so. Now if one were to draw a straight line between the low and inside pitch and the one high and away, the line would take a diagonal path. This point is ***key*** for your son to remember.

On the other hand, statistics have also shown that the two areas of real weakness for the left-handed batter. These are low and away, and high and inside. Similarly, these two areas of weakness can also be connected by a diagonal line.

So if your son wants to remember left-handed batters' strengths and weaknesses, all he has to do is remember just ***one area***, such as low and inside. Remembering that this hitter is strong here and in addition remembering the diagonal line relationship, he'll now know that the lefty is also strong high and away. Which leaves only two other areas that are this hitter's weaker pitches: low and away, and high and tight. By your son just remembering one area of strength for the left-handed batter, as well as the diagonal line relationship, he'll instantly also know this batter's other area of strength, as well as his two weaker hitting locations. This is reasoning simplicity at its best.

Now, the right-handed batter is the exact opposite to the lefty's strengths and weak hitting areas. But curiously, he's not actually that different. Suffice it to say, statistically the right-handed batter hits the ball low and away quite well. The diagonal line relationship holds up here equally well, so we now know from statistical analysis that he also hits the high and inside pitch pretty well too. But he is weaker high and away, as well as low and inside. And these two areas can also be connected by a diagonal line.

Now for the curiosity between lefties and righties.

The right hander's low and away area of strength is the very same locational area as the lefty's strength location; only the left-handed batter calls this pitch low and inside. The lefty's other strength is the high and away pitch, which is precisely the same other location of strength for the right-handed batter; only he calls it high and inside. So both areas are locations of strength for these batters, only that they simply name the areas differently.

Similarly, the areas of weakness for the right-hander is low and inside, which is also a weakness for the left-handed hitter, except he calls it low and away. Using the diagonal line, we know the righty is also weak high and away, as is the lefty. Except the lefty calls this area high and inside. This may be a curiosity of sorts, but how does knowing these coincidences help your son?

It's simple. If your son remembers just one area of strength for a batter, such as the lefty's low and inside pitch, then by using a diagonal line he also knows the lefty's other strong area. Your son will also be able to now identify this batter's two weak spots. But in addition and importantly, since he now knows that these areas are locationally identical both strong and weak spots for the right-handed batter (except that they're just named differently), he can also figure out the right-handed batter's area of both strength and weakness.

Thus by remembering only ***one*** batter's area of strength, as well as using the diagonal relationship principle, and knowing how left and right-handed batters match up locationally, your son can now pitch effectively to every batter he faces. He will know all of their natural areas of hitting strength and weakness.

Hands to the Ball

Too few young batters are ever taught to *take their hands to the ball.* This taking of the hands to the ball is a method of aiming the bat at the ball. This is made necessary because swinging a bat initiated from behind the batter's head and then bringing it around to make contact with a pitch out in front of the hitter is almost impossible to do. Unless a person leads with their hands first. This sort of aiming the bat is very much like the *steering wheel* of a car. Turn the hands and the car follows suit. So Major League ball players don't initially try to hit the ball with their bat. Rather, they try to hit the ball with their hands. They take their hands to where the ball will be, extend the bat and launch the ball.

So Watch the Batter's Hands

Your son should always be watching the swing to see whether the batter leads with his hands or the barrel of the bat. The batter should lead the hands into the contact zone first, then flex his, wrists which will bring the barrel of the bat around for contact. If he doesn't do this, your son will have an advantage.

Casting – A Pitcher's Advantage

Although a batter may swing the bat by leading the barrel to the ball before the hands, this kind of swing can only be successful on pitches thrown over the *outside corner* of the plate. But only sometimes. This type of swing is called *casting* because it resembles how one casts a fishing rod. But this batter will never make good contact with the *inside pitch* by casting at it and he'll have a similar problem with pitches over the middle of the plate.

The pitch on the *outside* corner can be hit 2-3 inches out in front of the plate and 2-3 inches deep into the plate. A pitch over the *middle* of the plate requires a batter making contact with the ball about 8 to 10 inches in front of the plate. And in order to hit the *inside* pitch, the batter must make contact with the ball 10-15 inches in front of the plate. (This assumes the batter's front foot is aligned with the front edge of the plate). So the only way to hit the pitches inside and over the middle of the plate is by keeping the hands close to the body and taking them to the ball, then extending the bat for solid contact. Recognizing the flaw of casting should help your son decide what pitches to throw to this batter.

And Watch the Batter's Swing

Have your son watch the batter's practice swings while at the plate. If he can, he could glance over to watch the batter swinging in the on-deck circle. And most importantly, watch the batter's hand motions as he swings at actual pitches. If this batter casts at the ball, your son knows his major weakness. He can't hit the inside pitch. The batter can never get the barrel of the bat into the contact zone when he casts his bat. And remember Dominant Hand Theory. This batter also begins with a natural weakness on the pitch low and inside. Strike two.

So What Pitches to Use?

If your son is a right hander, as this book assumes, then he may have three obvious choices of pitches to throw. The two-seam *sinker* is often the best pitch to use. It's a safe and easy pitch to execute and it can be thrown with both accuracy and velocity. The normal movement of this pitch will cause the ball, if thrown at about mid-plate, to then break inside and down on the batter. Ease of mechanics, velocity, and so much movement on the ball explains why this pitch is now the *newest best pitch* in the major leagues. Unlike the former best pitch, the *slider*, (which breaks down and away) the sinker won't hurt the elbow or shoulder. On the other hand, the slider, even when thrown properly, is guaranteed to injure ligaments around the elbow.

The *change-up* is another effective weapon to use against the batter who casts his bat. Most change-ups will break inside on a right-handed hitter. So batters who cast also have great difficulty with this pitch. But even if your son throws this pitch to a batter who does know how to keep his hands inside and take them to the ball, because the hitter has to start his swing so early in order to meet an inside pitch, this slower pitch often arrives *after* the bat has moved through the contact zone. The result is a swing and a miss. This pitch's lack of velocity is particularly effective against even a free swinging hitter who *doesn't* cast his bat.

The third pitch that can also be effective is your son's slower-end fastball. Most fastballs, when thrown with less than a hard effort, tend to have more movement from the pitcher's hand side to the glove side. So if your son's pitch moves the same way, have him practice throwing the ball at the batters thigh. The slower pitch should generate more glove side movement on the ball. As mentioned in an earlier chapter, this will cause it to break back across the inside corner of the plate for a strike. This is called a *backdoor pitch* and is often thrown around the thighs.

But never throw this or any other pitch around the batter's knees, just in case the pitch does not break back to the plate. No pitcher should intentionally throw at any batter and especially not at his knees. Even if a high pitch gets away and takes off towards a batter's head (Caution: Chronic Traumatic Encephalopathy (C.T.E.) Concussion Syndrome – Dave Duerson and Junior Seau. See Scientific American Feb. 2012 at P. 66.) the player can flop to avoid the pitch. But the knees can't be so easily moved out of the way. Catching a fastball on a knee can end a young player's career.

Understanding the why of Dominant Hand Theory

The reason the batter casts is because of his grip. When the hitter tries to swing, even by leading with his hands, he'll find that his top hand wants to take off out and away from the body. This occurs because the right hander's top hand in the grip is simply over powering his weaker left hand, which he wants to keep inside, close to the body, as it pulls the bat through the contact zone. But he can't. His upper right hand dominates the swing so much that it pushes the barrel to the outside of the plate. Once again, dominant hand theory explains why players cast and seldom are able to hit pitches on the inner half of the plate. It takes a lot of practice swings and much discipline to correct this bad habit.

One way to think of the physics at work in this swing is to imagine yourself exiting off of a long ramp on the highway. Because this road wraps around to the left, the centrifugal force starts to push your car outward to the curbside. You compensate by holding a firm hand on the steering wheel, which prevents the car from pitching off of the road. The other more common example may be the feeling of being flung off of a merry-go-round as it rotates. Again, centrifugal force at work.

This same centrifugal force is generated in a swing, causing the top of the hand to be thrown outside, much the way your car was. This is the same force that the batter has to overcome in his swing. Usually he can't. The dominant top hand drifts out and away from the body. In turn, it pulls the weaker left hand and bat with it. Like holding your car steady in the lane, batters are similarly challenged to keep their hands inside.

Converted Left-Handed Hitters

The dominant hand principle also explains why so many righties switch to the left side of the plate. By doing so, their dominant right hand drops to become the bottom hand of the grip. Now this dominant hand can more easily take the knob of the bat to the ball while at the same time overcoming the weaker left hand's urge to drift outside away from the body. This is the second reason why the low and inside pitch is an area of strength for the left-handed hitter. Switching hands also allows the left-handed batter to not only make more contact with inside pitches but also to hit with more power generated by the batter's dominant right hand pulling the bat through the contact zone.

Watch for the Upside-Down Grip

The occasional hitting coach will sometime have his player swing with an upside-down grip. This simply means that the right hander will reverse his hand positions so that his top right hand is moved to the bottom of the bat. This now leaves his left hand on top. This grip has the advantage of placing the dominant hand just above the knob of the bat, which allows the right hand to guide the knob with a push and the left hand now pulls from the top. With the right hand leading the way, the batter can now more easily keep his hands inside and thus be able to hit the inside pitch. This batter, if he can make the adjustment, will be able to hit both inside and outside pitches. But seldom with any power. This grip produces the classic contact hitter.

Your son can still confuse this batter by mixing up his pitches. But even if he is hit, it won't be hard. Just have him remember that this right-hander now has both the same location strengths and weaknesses as a left-handed batter. Your son should continue to just mix up pitches, speed, and location.

Full Count Pitches

Whether this batter is a free-swinging, aggressive power hitter or just a player who normally looks to make contact in this count, almost every young player is sitting on a fastball. Most pitchers are taught to throw their best pitch in this count and this usually means your son's fastball. And the batters know this. But there's nothing wrong with your son using this strategy and going head to head with his best pitch, up against a hard swinging batter. Remember that this batter will still have to execute his swing properly in order to hit this pitch. This is never an easy thing to do. But this doesn't have to be your son's only strategy.

My son was in a 3-2 count and threw two fastballs, both high in the zone. Each time the batter fouled off the ball. So I called out, "Jeremy, what just happened to the last two pitches? Now decide what you're going to throw." Jeremy came set and then threw. The batter swung and the ball harmlessly floated over the plate for a strike. Jeremy had chosen properly and threw his change-up across the middle of the plate while the batter's swing was way too early. The change-up was not Jeremy's best pitch, but it was a pitch that he could always throw for strikes. Many young players simply need to find the courage to throw their own change-up more often. Pure velocity is not everything.

This scenario simply illustrates that even when the fastball is your son's best pitch, his second best pitch may prove to be equally effective. Particularly in situations like this when the batter has just seen his fastball and is getting his timing down. This is when an off-speed pitch can be most effective.

Besides, walking batters is not the end of the world. If it's the bottom of the last inning and the bases are loaded, it may be the end of the game. But it's never the end of the world. Even if a game is lost, it's still only a game. Most young players, and too often older ones as well, don't realize that Lombardi was wrong. Winning is only really important in war. Thankfully baseball is just a kid's game. So your son should compete, have some fun and enjoy the game. Winning the game takes a back seat to each of these goals.

A Batter Who Doesn't Watch T.V.

So many young batters don't know how to watch a pitched ball. If your son looks down at a batter and the hitter's head is ***not*** fully turned, then he's not looking back at your son with ***both*** of his eyes, and your son has an advantage. And again dominant hand theory has a role to play.

In order to ***see*** the pitch properly the batter must turn his entire ***face*** to look over his front shoulder. In this position, both of the hitter's eyes can focus on the pitch and make judgment calls. This is called having a ***T.V. face*** because that's the head position which most of us use when watching T.V. This face-forward position allows us to use both eyes when watching our programs and judge depth and movement accurately. This is how the better hitters watch the pitcher.

However, the unskilled hitter will often only turn his head halfway around to look at the pitcher. In this case, he is focusing mostly with just his left eye. Worse still, this is the weaker of his two eyes. His dominant and stronger eye is his right eye, which can't quite see the pitcher clearly nor properly track the ball's movement. Your son should take advantage of this weakness.

Actually, this kind of batter can't see any pitch really well. But due to velocity changes and ball movement, this batter has a real problem hitting the breaking pitches. Particularly when an occasional fastball is thrown into the mix. Since the batter with a T.V. face just can't use both of his eyes to focus on the pitch, this makes judging speed, depth, and movement an almost impossible challenge. So just by looking at the batter's face your son can determine how he'll pitch to him. Television watching will never be quite the same again for your son.

The Batter's Feet Placement

The batter who moves up in the batter's box wants to edge closer to your son. The hitter is trying to get to your son's breaking pitches but before they break. He's usually looking for the curveball. This way the pitch will be a slower moving one but not yet with all the movement it has when it breaks down over the plate.

The answer to this batter's strategy is to simply bust him with fastballs. It'll be particularly effective if your son can throw this pitch on the inside corner. Now the batter will really have to start his bat early, if he means to jump on this pitch. Usually he can't.

The batter who moves to the back of the plate is hoping to have more time to react to your son's fastball. The extra foot he gains from standing here allows him a longer time to see and judge this pitch. But this batter is now susceptible to your son's breaking pitches, particularly his curveball. The curve should start to dive to the ground just out in front of the plate. A well-thrown curve could end up around this batter's ankles by the time it reaches him. Seldom does a batter swing at such a pitch and then get a called strike. If he does swing, this ball is often only golfed into the air for an easy out. Both the breaking change-up and your son's sinker can also present real timing and movement problems for a hitter sitting on the fastball, when standing further back in the batter's box. So just remind your son to check the batter's foot placement before he decides what to throw.

Look for a Check Mark

The best and easiest way to hit a baseball is by taking the hands down into the contact zone early and then level the hands and bat on a line parallel to the ground. As the swing continues, the batter initiates solid contact with the ball and then, and only then, he pulls the hands and bat out and away from the contact zone. This is called *Getting in early, stay long and get out late* or, *in early, out late*.

By executing this type of swing the batter has a better chance of seeing the ball and adjusting his bat swing to the best contact position, as well as generating the maximum amount of contact. This swing will also produce more power. However, most young batters *can't* do this. They just haven't been properly trained.

Instead, many batters have what is called a *check mark swing*. This refers to the batter taking his hands (and bat) into the strike zone too *late* and then he pulls out too *early*. This motion resembles the look of a check mark.

To some extent this undisciplined stroke is the result of *waiting on the pitch* too long, rather than having the confidence to *anticipate*. And then, trying to hit the ball too hard rather than *staying on the ball* with the bat to just make solid contact. This would then require the defense to react and play some ball.

If your son recognizes a check mark swinger, his most effective pitches should be his breaking balls. A check mark hitter can sometimes get lucky and time the fastball just right. But your son's breaking pitches are more difficult to find with this kind of swing, simply because the ball is moving sideways so much. So your son should work the batter with breaking pitches but keep him off balance with the occasional fastball. A fastball thrown high, even out of the strike zone, cannot be hit by a check mark batter. But it will still throw off the batter's timing for breaking pitches. Remember watch the batter swing!

The Puller

A lot of power hitters make the common mistake of *pulling off the ball*. Because they want to hit with as much power as possible, by not controlling their body properly they swing too hard, lose their mechanics and fall away (backwards) from the pitches' flight path. And even if this batter takes his hands to the ball properly and gets in early and stays late, because he pulls his body around so hard, he still ends up pulling his bat away from the pitch.

Your son will easily recognize this type of hitter by simply watching whether the batter spins his body, much like that of a toy spinning top. What is happening is the hitter is pulling his front shoulder back and away from the plate. This results in his also pulling his bat out of the contact zone and away from the pitches.

This batter may well be able to hit the inside pitch but he's very vulnerable on the outside corner. So your son should throw both fastballs and breaking pitches to the outside corner of the plate. But watch to see if the batter tries to adjust, by moving his feet closer to the plate, so he can reach these pitches. If he does, bust him back inside with a fastball or sinker. Both pitches can eat this batter up and force him to move back away from the plate. Now have your son go away to the outside corner again, with all of his pitches. Just remind him to watch the batter's feet as the hitter tries to adjust to your son's location.

Destroy the Batter's Rhythm

The more your son pitches, the sooner he will find a rhythm for pitching. He'll receive the ball from his catcher, turn and get set to look in for the sign, then start his windup and throw. This rhythm will become a habit and he'll begin to feel comfortable with it. Most pitchers pitch with a rhythm, but they shouldn't always do this, if they can help it.

Because your son's rhythm will soon become the batter's rhythm. He'll get used to your son's habits and he'll use this rhythm to help himself become comfortable. This will help him to time your son's pitches, and this is never good for a pitcher. Your son has to make the batter uncomfortable and he can do this by denying the hitter a pitcher's rhythm to feed off of, and then by destroying the batter's own rhythm.

Your son should constantly disrupt his opponent's rhythm by taking longer to receive the catcher's signs. The pitcher can pause and look over to the on-deck circle. He can stare in at the signs longer than he needs to (just make sure the catcher knows what he's doing). Your son can then step off the rubber and start again. And for the next pitch he can speed everything up and try to pitch more quickly. Any and all of these techniques can be used to upset the batter's sense of comfort. Hopefully these delay tactics will also cause the batter's arms and body to tighten up, which should slow down his swing.

However, two points are worth mentioning. Your son shouldn't use these tactics against every batter. He should save them for the better batters or for the more important situations. Otherwise his opponents will figure him out.

Second, the umpire may not let him use all of these techniques. They're not illegal (except for a clear *quick pitch*) but the umpire may call time out to caution the pitcher to move the game along. Remember a clear (constant) delay of game, is an infraction. But your son will be warned once before the umpire calls it.

The most important message is that a batter likes to find a comfort zone and establish a rhythm. Your son shouldn't help him and he should try to upset the hitter's own rhythm in any way he can.

A final caution. If all of this tinkering hurts your son's pitching performance, he should forget about it for now. It will simply be too much, too soon.

A Hitting Pitcher

This chapter has focused upon teaching your son how to recognize a hitter's weaknesses and then take advantage of them. If your son wants to learn how to recognize defects in a batter's swing, the best way for him to do this is for him to learn how to hit properly himself. Finding a hitting coach or sending your son off to a reputable baseball camp would not only improve the hitting dimension of his game but it would also improve upon his pitching ability. Your son can develop further pitching strategies based upon what he learns about proper hitting. Besides, he'd have some fun at camp while he's learning. And that's what the game of baseball is really all about.

CHAPTER 5
THE EMOTIONAL GAME

Pitching's Three Elements

Successful pitching relies upon a player's ability to execute three elements of his game. If he is to master his potential, he must master the physical, the mental, and the emotional challenges confronting him during a game.

The physical challenges are addressed in the early chapter on mechanics. They are the foundation for all pitchers. The majority of a young player's time should be spent on developing an ability to throw pitches properly. Unless your son can do this, he will not be able to capitalize on the mental aspect of the game.

The mental or strategic side of the game was addressed in the last chapter on creating a game plan. It involves an understanding of both pitching principles and tactics. Knowledge of how to make physical adjustments during the game will simply complement your son's ability to make use of this knowledge.

Yet there is more to successful pitching than just knowing what pitch to throw and having the physical ability to throw it. Your son also needs to have ***the desire*** to throw the ball in every count.

THE TEST

Imagine that you're a young pitcher in a big game with the runners on first and second. Their big hitter comes to bat and on your first pitch, he takes you out of the park. Now what do you do? This is the dilemma faced by every pitcher, at every level of baseball, at some time during his career. How your son handles himself in these circumstances will determine how successful his pitching career will progress.

A player may have terrific control of four pitches, high end velocity, and a sound grasp of pitching strategy. But unless he also can control his emotions under stress, then these other tools will be of little usefulness. Fear, distraction, and uncertainty can all combine to upset your son's ability to execute his next pitch. If he becomes afraid of being hit again, his body will tense up and he won't be able to execute his pitches properly. He'll lose both velocity and control. In fact, some players won't throw into the strike zone, even if their physical tools are working properly. Simply because they're afraid of being hit. In essence, emotional control lies at the heart of pitching success.

Believe in Self

This book has provided your son a number of tools that he can use in a game.

But these tools won't be of any use if your son doesn't have the confidence in himself to use them. Effective pitching begins and ends with self-confidence. Your son has to believe in himself, his abilities and his decisions. If he has any doubts about himself as a pitcher then this doubt will find its way into his pitching performance. When he's hit or walks a batter, this self-doubt will grow and there will be no possibility for him to pitch to his capabilities. His opportunity on this day, at least, will be lost. As a parent you can help foster confidence and perhaps even a little tough-mindedness in your son. Both will be helpful when he becomes faced with challenges, as he surely will. Being with him at games and practices, if possible, will help. Share his moments of success and failure. Encourage the first and ensure that he can walk away from the second with his head held high.

Vince Lombardi once said, "Winning isn't everything, it's the only thing". Well, he was wrong, because winning is only truly important in war. These are just youth baseball games and your son should never let any loss affect him any more than that.

Confidence

The ability to continue throwing strikes, even after being hit hard, is firmly based on a player's confidence in himself. A successful pitcher simply believes enough in his own abilities that he will get the batter out. Football great, Johnny Unitas, had this to say about confidence:

> There is a difference between conceit and confidence. A quarterback (like a pitcher) has to have confidence. Conceit is bragging about yourself. Confidence means you believe you can get the job done. I have always believed that I could get the job done.

The ability to continue throwing strikes, even after being hit hard, is firmly based upon a player's confidence in himself. A successful pitcher simply believes enough in his own abilities that he will get the batter out, even after his best pitch has been taken for a ride.

Preparation

Confidence, in most cases, finds its own origins in the success which a pitcher has had in the past. A history of success always breeds confidence in the ability to have more successes. But what happens when a young pitcher hasn't had much success, because he has just begun to pitch? How can he become confident when he has no track record to feel confident about? Part of the answer lies in a quote of former basketball great David Robinson. Robinson observed that,

> I'm going to be a success at whatever I choose because of my preparation. By the time the game starts, the outcome has been decided. I never think about having a bad game because I have prepared.

This is the answer for pitchers who haven't yet had a lot of game success. It is also equally effective for those successful pitchers who want to keep on enjoying the success that they've already experienced. If a pitcher prepares thoroughly by practicing his pitches, refining his mechanics, and working at all of his skill drills, then he will be as prepared as possible to face the batters. Knowing that he's done all that he can do to be ready to play will allow him to relax and be confident in his performance, simply because he knows that there's nothing more that he can do and he's as ready as he can possibly be.

Advantages of Confidence

Pitching with confidence has two distinct advantages. Firstly, it permits a player to physically relax. Secondly, it also allows a player to easily maintain his focus on the job at hand. Physical relaxation is vital for a pitcher. If he is scared or tense, his body will tighten up. In turn, this tightness will prevent him from maintaining smooth mechanics throughout his delivery. The result will be a loss of both location as well as his velocity. Pitches will either stay up or miss the strike zone entirely.

In addition to physical relaxation, confidence permits a player to keep his mind on the task at hand. Because he's relaxed he will more easily be able to consider his options with his batter. For example,

- Is he crowding the plate?
- Is he stepping in the bucket?
- Is he taking a long stride?
- Is he taking long looping swings?
- Is he setting his front elbow at his shoulders?
- Are there runners on base and what's the score and inning?
- Now what tactic or strategy should be employed?

All of these assessments will be made more easily and the resulting decision arrived at simply because your son's confidence has allowed him to relax and think about what to throw next.

Be Calm and Focused

Essentially what confidence provides the player is the mental state of *relaxation* or *calmness*. The emotional state of calm permits him to perform both physically and mentally at his optimum level. Both your son's record of success and his ability to *prepare* will help him attain this state of relaxation. However there are a few other techniques that he may wish to try that have already had a *record of success* with many major league pitchers.

Breathing

Something as simple as proper breathing will help your son to relax. Dorfman describes it this way:

> To use the race car metaphor once again, carbon dioxide acts as a break; oxygen acts as an accelerator. Carbon dioxide slams down muscles; oxygen propels them smoothly. When exhaling deeply, pitchers release carbon dioxide from their blood stream and allow oxygen to take over.

Your son's muscles will then relax as they release the tension from his body. Both his mind and body will be better able to perform in a fluid and efficient manner. Taking a deep breath in through the nose and then exhaling from the mouth should become a regular habit before every pitch. Certainly before every important pitch.

SELF-COACHING

Self-coaching is another calming technique used by many major league pitchers. Perhaps Mark "The Bird" Fidrych is the most well-known practitioner of this skill. Fidrych would actually hold the ball up to his face and tell it where he wanted it to go on the next pitch. Although this was the Bird's approach, your son doesn't have to be quite so dramatic.

Before every pitch your son may wish to think to himself what he wants to do next. For example, he may wish to say to himself, "Let's keep the body down the line and really reach at the release point." Or, "Stay tall and compact, and reach to that target." The goal is to make sure that he's very specifically focused on that one objective. This kind of self-coaching helps to achieve this kind of focus.

But some pitchers don't self-coach for every pitch. They feel that when things are going well, they prefer to not do anything to break or slow down their rhythm. Instead they use this technique of talking themselves to a successful pitch only when things are not what they should be. Then self-coaching can bring them back to a relaxed and focused state of mind. In these instances, this pitcher will often call timeout, step off of the mound and rub down the ball. Then he'll self-coach the desired results he's looking for, step back up on the mound, and go back to work. Watch for this pattern the next time you and your son take in a major league game. It's used all the time.

Mantra

Using a *mantra* is very similar to self-coaching, except that the directions or words are not quite so specific to each pitching circumstance. In fact, a mantra is more like a chant than anything else.

This chant has been likened to a form of brainwashing because of how it works. The pitcher will decide that he wants to have a mantra for two or three specific circumstances. For example, often a pitcher will want to refocus his mind on his execution of the next pitch. He needs to be 100 percent focused on this pitch. So he may choose to use the mantra, "This pitch," or "Right here." Repeating this phrase two or three times will help him eliminate all other distractions and re-focus everything he has on the next pitch. And by employing this technique time and again, his ability to refocus his concentration becomes even that much easier. In this way some have compared it to a type of self-brainwashing. Actually it's more closely linked to a form of self-hypnosis.

Your son should also recognize that he can develop a few mantras, each designed to address a specific goal. For example, periodically Jeremy will want to ensure that he stays loose and flexible, so as to enhance his delivery. Sometimes a pitcher will start to tighten up without recognizing it, and this tightness can interfere with his execution of a quality pitch. So throughout the game he will occasionally repeat to himself "Be Gumby." In this way, his subconscious will recognize the predetermined suggestion that he has given himself, to stay loose and fluid in his delivery just like the Gumby cartoon character.

You and your son should discuss what mantras will help him perform at his optimum level. When doing this there are a few key ideas to remember. First, keep the chant short. Remember it's a chant not a poem. Second, always use a positive suggestion. Avoid negatives like, "Don't miss" or "Don't walk him." These don't work and commonly produce the very result he wanted to avoid. Also, find a mantra and stick to it. He shouldn't bounce from one to another hoping to see which one works best. They will all work, but he has to give the suggestion time to take in the subconscious. So find one and stick with it.

But make sure it's really *his* mantra. A parent may have a great idea for a mantra but if his son doesn't really care for it, forget it. Remember, it's his subconscious that has to be stimulated, so he has to work with a phrase that keys something inside of him. You may be able to help with ideas for a chant, but the final decision has to be his. And lastly, he shouldn't have more than two or three mantras. He should just pick a couple of very specific responses that he's trying to elicit, such as bringing all of his focus and attention to this next pitch. Too many mantras only dilutes the strength of each suggestion. So find the most important part of his game that needs his primary attention and develop a mantra to fix that problem. Add one more and he's probably good to go.

Possible Pitcher's Mantra

Right on the corner
Hard inside
Inflate my chest and take it home
The closer I am to the plate the less time they have to react
Stride long, pitch long
Everything down the line
My head leads the way
All pitches – reach A to B, then hand speed
Extend the arm, now quicken the release

Changing Mantras

Your son must come up with a mantra he feels comfortable with. If he has doubts, the following constitute commonly used mantras.

Right on the corner
Hard inside
Inflate my chest and take it home
The closer I am to the plate the less time they have to
react
Stride long, pitch long
My backside follows my front side
Everything down the line
Extend the arm to the box, now quick release

All pitches – reach A to B, then hand speed
My head leads the way
This is a walk in the park
Trust, and just throw
Force him to hit my pitch
I always have the advantage
A to B – reach – then hand speed

VISUALIZATION

Visualization is another method of *keying the subconscious* in a way that will help your son to perform. The idea is for him to visualize in *his mind's eye* the results that he would like to produce on the field.

For example, if he wants to maximize the speed of his throwing arm in order to produce more velocity, he could visualize himself pitching and his arm moving so fast that it's almost too fast to actually see. It's moving with a blur. The key here is to exaggerate the results he wants to produce. This *symbolic* gesture will stimulate his subconscious so that if his mind is holding his arm speed down, it'll get the message to stop holding him back. Instead he'll now perform up to his full capability.

He can also use visualization to help improve his *location.* He should visualize seeing himself from the umpire's position or perhaps from behind the mound. From either vantage point, he should see the ball leaving his hand (as the pitcher) and hitting the exact spots he'll be aiming for during the game. This may be a fastball low on the outside corner, or a change-up just floating into the low inside position. Also, visualizing a low curveball breaking away towards the outside corner may be another exercise he may wish to try. This kind of *visualization for results* has also been used in other sports with great success.

Visualization can help your son with other parts of his delivery. Just as he watches himself in a mirror while performing balance points, similarly he should visualize his entire pitching delivery. He should begin by seeing himself pitching slowly with all of his body parts being in the right place, at the right time. He can see his tall, balanced body take a rocker step backwards, the solid foot plant, the hands separating to where he wants them to go, a hard rotation, a stride and knee pull, and then the decelerating arm. Your son should focus on whatever area he thinks needs his attention the most. He should just see a solid delivery, the way he would like his body to perform. Now gradually speed up the delivery to game conditions. Once again, he will be teaching his *unconscious mind* the way he wants his body to move.

With Eyes Closed and Open

Initially your son will have to start his visualizing program with his eyes closed. Obviously it's easier to avoid distractions by doing it this way. For a few minutes every day, he should find a quiet comfortable place to sit and just visualize himself performing those elements of his game that he wants to improve. Jeremy would also visualize his goals the morning of game day or even in the car on the way to the park.

Once your son has made this a daily routine, he'll soon be able to move quickly and more vividly to the areas he wants to work on. But soon he'll realize that he can actually visualize these drills in his mind's eye, even with his eyes open. His ability to focus will have moved to the next level, and he'll realize that he now has another important tool to use.

For example, while sitting on the bench he can visualize seeing himself loose and limber, pitching off that actual day's mound. He no longer needs to find that quiet room to perform this task. Better still, your son can now add visualizing to his tools on the mound. If his location is giving him a problem, have him call time out. He should step off of the mound and begin to wipe down the ball. As he's doing this, he should visualize seeing the next pitch hitting his catcher's glove in the exact spot he wants it to. This should take only a few seconds. Now he can step back up on the mound and go back to work.

Cool and Calm vs. Mean Streak

What has been described earlier in this chapter applies to both the pitcher whose temperament is cool and calm or that of a more emotional and aggressive pitcher. Sometimes referred to as bordering on having a mean streak. Both approaches are represented in the Major League today, so obviously both can be successful.

The cool, calculating pitcher will almost always have his emotions in check and pitch almost dispassionately. He has a game plan, knows how to react in different situations and has almost workman-like way about him. The more aggressive pitcher can be readily seen talking to himself, muttering something in the direction of the opponent's dugout and occasionally tossing the rosin bag around the mound. This is a pitcher who may just as well have the same game plan and knowledge of pitch count situations, as does the more laid back pitcher. But this pitcher attacks the mound and the batters with a purpose. And yet, both kinds of pitchers can be successful.

Some of the laid-back pitchers occasionally have to be encouraged to develop a competitor's edge. Not nastiness, the pitches will do that. Just a little more "get after him" in certain game situations. Jeremy used to listen to Eminem's song Lose Yourself before every game just to give himself that extra edge he thought that he needed.

On the other hand, the aggressive pitcher sometimes has to be cooled off, particularly when all about him things are falling apart. He has to learn that the shortstop won't improve his next throw to first base because the pitcher has turned and barked at him. Sometimes these emotions have to be restrained and he be reminded to go back to work.

But each approach can make for a successful pitcher. Your son should be encouraged to evolve into the kind of pitcher which best suites his personality. What should not happen is a parent trying to turn his son's temperament into that of a major leaguer he has seen on T.V. Not only won't this work but it will probably only succeed in driving his son away from the game.

Feeling Comfortable

All of this chapter has been dedicated to one thing: finding a way for your son to be comfortable on the mound. Coaches or fans who yell criticisms or words like "don't" at the pitcher don't realize that they're doing more harm than good. Negative thoughts are the last thing that any pitcher needs to hear when he's competing. They only serve to annoy him and tighten up his body. Once the body tightens up, there go the mechanics. Then the pitches start missing their spots and begin hanging in places that they shouldn't. Things only go from bad to worse. What the pitcher needs is a feeling of comfort. This will be achieved with positive words of encouragement that help your son simply feel comfortable and relaxed on the mound. Other techniques may also be used but everything must focus upon what he wants to happen.

Routine

Even something as simple as performing the same specific routine over and over again can help your son find his focus and in doing so, help to calm him down. For example, at the beginning of every inning of every game, Jeremy performs the same simple routine. After taking his warm-up pitches, he steps off of the mound and begins. First he throws the ball into his glove, then takes his cap off, wipes his forehead with the back of the glove, puts the cap back on from front to back, rubs down the ball, licks his two throwing fingers, wipes them on his pant leg, and finally steps back up on the mound. He then steps on the rubber and takes a big breath, slowly exhales and looks in for his catcher's signal. He's now ready to go. He may or may not self-coach or visualize something specific while he's performing this routine. It depends upon the circumstances. But the real advantage for him is just this little routine.

This routine calms his emotions and focuses his mind so that he's now ready to pitch. If there were any other distractions from the crowd or random thoughts running through his mind, this little routine erases all of this. Because he has used this routine every game, for so many years, the transformation to a calm and focused pitcher is now instantaneous. This routine has communicated to his subconscious the need for relaxation and focus. And because he's done it so many times before, the subconscious knows exactly what to do.

Routine – Especially in Tough Circumstances

Jeremy will also use this routine when things aren't going well or it's a critical point in the game. In these situations, he'll call timeout to self-coach or visualize. But before stepping immediately back on the mound, he'll use this *routine* to provide himself with the calm and focus, which he'll need. Your son too, should consider establishing a routine that he can use on game day. It can be a very quick and effective way for him to get ready to pitch.

A Positive Frame of Mind

Your son will find that maintaining a positive frame of mind is a valuable tool for producing successful results. When self-coaching or reciting a mantra, he must ensure that his words are always of a positive nature. Negative suggestions like "don't miss" or "don't walk him," are never as effective as the positive alternative. Like, "right on the corner" or "he's going down." As mentioned earlier, suggestions which incorporate a negative idea never produce the success of a positively worded phrase. And often, they produce exactly the opposite results one is searching for.

A positive frame of mind energizes both the psyche and the body. A negative viewpoint saps the life right out of a player. Self-doubt can also very easily lead to fear. And fear will inevitably cause your son's muscles to tighten up. Not only will he not be able to execute his pitches properly, but any consequential negative result (walks, hits, etc.) will only convince him that his fear was well deserved. This will only breed further self-doubt and failure. The way to prevent this from occurring is by maintaining a positive frame of mind at all times.

Proper Perspective

Keeping a positive attitude, particularly when things aren't going well, takes practice just like anything else. This can be assisted by his always remembering to keep a positive perspective on the game and never give it more value than it deserves. After all, it is only that: just a game. No one's life is at stake. No one is getting a shoe deal out of this, nor are the losers being sent to jail. It's just a game. And the purpose of every game that I'm aware of is to have fun. So remind your son that he shouldn't overreact to whatever happens and just keep things in their proper perspective.

Proper Evaluation

If your son is going to be bothered by something, he should at least be sure that he's being bothered about something that he can affect. So make sure that he's looking at his *behavior* in the play, *not* the final *consequences* of the play. This means that if your son's pitch went exactly where he wanted to put the ball, and the pitch both moved with the intended velocity as well as break, then he just threw a great pitch. He achieved the exact *behavior* that he was looking for. The fact that the batter took it out of the park does absolutely nothing to minimize the success of your son's behavior. Understanding this distinction is crucial.

Perhaps the batter did a great *job* in executing *his job* or maybe he just guessed right. On the other hand, perhaps your son's *choice of pitch* was not the right one to throw in those circumstances. But no matter why the batter was successful, it's important that your son understand that he was in fact successful in executing his pitch. The ball moved to the intended location, with both the velocity and movement that he wanted to impart to the ball. This pitch then must be recognized for what it is: a successful pitch.

It's always important for your son to learn from the consequences of his behavior but he mustn't confuse the two. He can affect his own behavior, but not the consequences of this behavior. That's up to others to determine. For example, if your son wanted to induce a pop fly or ground ball, but the infielder misplayed the ball and the runner was safe at first, your son must realize that he did his job. His goal was a certain *behavior* and he accomplished it. The *consequences* of his behavior are not up to him. Your son should understand that it is only his own behavior that he can control, so this is how he should focus his efforts. And not be distracted by consequences.

So your son must set his own goals of behavior. This could be throwing strikes and low pitches, or executing proper mechanics and minimizing walked batters. Whether the ground ball is misplaced or the team loses the game, are consequences that he can surely learn from (e.g. don't throw soft pitches inside). But they are not standards by which he should evaluate his own performance.

Learn from the Bad

Your son should take very opportunity to learn from things that go wrong. If all of his low pitches to a batter are being hit, he has to realize that he may have just run into a pure low-ball hitter. What is the batter doing with his swing that might have tipped off your son to this fact? How should he pitch to this guy? Maybe this kind of stance or swing will tip off your son to other low ball hitters, and give him a heads-up on how to get them out in the next game.

In an earlier chapter, it was described how Jeremy threw a low-end fastball that was fouled off, followed by a curve for a called strike and then a change-up. When his third pitch was knocked out of the park, he later realized that he can't throw a change-up behind two soft pitches. He never will again. It was the only time that season that he had been hit hard. But rather than get down on himself, he found the positive lesson in a bad situation.

It's important that your son too realize that by evaluating his performance after each game, he can acquire valuable knowledge to be used in the next game. Understanding that a disappointing outing can still produce positive results, should help to keep him looking at his performance with a positive attitude

Poise

Combining the ability to concentrate while maintaining a positive outlook produces what all coaches are looking for: poise. ***Poise*** is the ability to be at ease in any situation but most particularly when things are going wrong. It means simply being in control of one's emotions.

Baseball coaches commonly talk about poise when offering their advice to pitchers that they should always *maintain high lows and low highs*. A pitcher should avoid getting overly excited by his success, just as much as he should avoid allowing his failures to get him down. Both the emotions of excitement and disappointment can interfere with a pitcher's ability to focus or execute his pitches. Brian Sipe describes it this way:

> The only way to maximize potential for performance is to be calm in the mind.

Coach Dale Brown described it this way:

> The masters all have the ability to discipline themselves to eliminate everything except what they are trying to accomplish.

There is no better example of a pitcher who has mastered the disposition of poise than Greg Maddux. No pitcher better exemplifies the ability to always keep his emotions in check. Whether he has just thrown the winning pitch or the ball just went for a ride into the bleachers, his on-field emotional response is always the same. He's calm and in control of his emotions. He leaves his celebrations or disappointments for later.

But what's so wrong with a little on-field celebration after having just gotten a big out? Provided that it's not done to excess and crossed the line of poor sportsmanship. Perhaps nothing, in itself. But the problem doesn't actually occur when a player fails to hold his emotions in check in order to celebrate his *success*. Rather, the problem arises when this pitcher has a *failure*. If his emotions can't be restrained and controlled when the player has a success, you can be absolutely guaranteed that he won't be able to control them when he faces adversity. Now the negative emotions set in. Doubt, hesitation, fear of failure, and so on, will all take over this pitcher's performance. And the results won't be good.

Focusing on keeping *high lows and low highs*, will provide your son with the necessary poise which he'll need to always be in control of his game. And when he's proud of something he's done, just remind him of what Coach Terry Bawden said:

> "When it comes to celebrating, act like you've been there before."

Discipline

Success at anything in life whether it is sport, academics, business, family life or even one's social skills, is chiefly reliant upon discipline. Certainly one's success with pitching is no different from these other endeavors. So your son's pitching success is going to be directly tied to his aptitude for self-discipline.

It only makes sense that discipline will play such an integral role in your son's pitching success. It's his discipline that will help him to:

- Achieve poise
- High lows and low highs
- Establish a positive frame of mind
- Getting to practice
- Performing his drills
- Keeping the proper perspective
- Dealing with disappointments
- Pitching through adversity
- Make all the necessary sacrifices required to excel

As Coach Lou Halty said:

> "Without self-discipline, success is impossible, period!"

But establishing a foundation for self-discipline, particularly at a young age, isn't always so easy to achieve. In fact, it will usually take a parent's own self-discipline to help establish that of his son. For example, if your son gets to all his practices and performs all of his drills, it's probably because you were disciplined enough to be the person driving the car and working out with him. And it will take your observations and reminders of the value of strategies, mechanics, pitching values and so forth that will encourage him with the necessary motivation to develop his own habits and discipline.

You can help further by ensuring that the game always remains fun. Creating drills that can mimic challenges and games in themselves will also help. Although performing drills can be boring and sometimes very tedious, if you can show him how the results will provide him with some fun down the road, this will often help him to persevere. And along the way, without being aware of it, he'll be creating the foundation for the discipline, which is so necessary for him in establishing his pitching success.

The Game Plan

Just having a game plan will provide your son confidence simply by his knowing that he's already ahead of his opponents. This knowledge should help him to relax physically as well as mentally and stay focused on the task at hand. But your son has to believe in his game plan if he expects to execute it successfully.

Having any doubts about it reduces it to little more than just a pitch-by-pitch series of choices. If your son loses confidence in his game plan then he loses the opportunity to pitch using his own choices. So once he chooses his strategy for the game he has to stay true to it. Trust it and it will produce results.

Sample Game Plan

1. Pre-game psyche: find music or writing that can he which he can use to develop an edge. Michael Jordan use to listen to Anita Baker's "Giving You the Best That I got" before games.
2. Get warm-ups in early
3. Breath -Always
4. Innings 1 and 2 -Pitch hard to soft
5. Inning 3 -Pitch soft to hard
6. Inning 4, 5 and 6 –Alternate Innings
7. Utilize Dominant Hand Theory with unknowns
8. Remember #7 with big hitters
9. Watch the Batter – Watch the Swing.
10. Adjust and Breath!
11. Don't let baserunners distract from primary job.

PITCHING WITH A RUNNER

As described earlier in this book, the most important thing for your son to understand is that it is not his goal to pick the runner off of the base. The term "pick-off move" is perhaps the biggest misnomer in all of baseball. The array of actions used to "pick off" the runner whether it's looking over, stepping off, delaying his delivery and even the actual throw to the bas, are not actually intended to pick off the runner. Only in exceptional instances, when the runner is surprised, is the pitcher ever successful in picking off the baserunner. The actual intent of all of these moves is simply to hold the runner close to the bag. This way if the batter makes contact the runner won't get a good jump on the ball and be able to take that extra base or even score.

So this being the case does it make any sense for your son to be at all distracted by the runner. Of course not. Now this doesn't mean that your son should completely ignore the baserunner. Yes he should step off occasionally and even sometimes make a throw to the bag. But your son must not become so preoccupied by the baserunner that his focus on the hitter is distracted. His first and foremost priority is always the batter. If your son is successful in getting each and every batter out, then no runs will score. The baserunner can steal his way to third base but he will be left there if your son focuses on the job at hand. And this is always getting the batter out.

College Souting and Recruiting

As your son moves through high school playing baseball, many young people consider moving to the next level with their game. This topic is considered at some length in another book by this author. So only a couple of matters will be discussed here.

Being Seen by College Coaches

Club or *travel teams* have been the most popular vehicle for young players to be viewed by college coaches. However, although these teams are a useful way to be scouted, times are changing. Arguably, they are no longer the best way to be seen. But this can only be truly appreciated by first understanding the schools' financial limitations.

Unlike other college sports, most notably football and basketball, baseball teams have very little money available to be spent on scouting for players. NCAA Division I schools permit each school to fund only a total of 11.7 athletic scholarships, per team, per year. That means that teams that commonly carry over thirty players must divide these scholarship finds among the entire team. Consequently it is almost of unheard of for any player to receive a *full ride*. Usually those players who receive any money at all often receive a scholarship between 20 and 60 percent of their total academic costs. Usually about half of the team are *walk-on* players who receive no athletic money at all. As you can well imagine, these coaches similarly have a very limited budget for scouting players. And traveling to tournaments to scout unknown products is an expense that few teams can now afford.

College coaches have responded by improvising. Many schools enter into loose agreements among themselves to share costs and information. So schools like Harvard and MIT will agree to share information each collects on players that they see. In this way expenses can be minimized, while knowledge can be maximized. But the most important change that you and your son must be aware of is the use of *prospect camps* for scouting players. They have changed the face of college recruiting for baseball.

Club Team Limitations

Many club teams will advertise the exhibition games and tournaments that they will attend. A team may attend *showcase tournaments* over the winter and spring breaks, as well as two or three each summer. But exactly which schools and coaches will be in attendance? Although the club team coaches are often told by tournament organizers that certain college coaches will be in attendance, often these promises are not accurately reflected with bodies in the stands. Not every coach who is *invited* by the organizers actually attend. But the club coaches have no way of knowing this. They can only hope for the best.

But club team players have other problems as well. What if your son wants to attend any one of three or four schools, but none of them are at these tournaments? Or, what if your son isn't scheduled to pitch on the day your son's ideal school is watching? Or, what if he has only a mediocre performance that day, which doesn't truly reflect his real potential? Fortunately, all coaches look for pitchers. But if your son was a first baseman and his favorite school's coach was in attendance, what if he already has two top-line first baseman? This year he's looking for middle infielders. Usually there are few positive answers that club teams can provide these players. But prospect camps offer answers and a positive alternative to all of these problems.

Prospect Camps

Every year, many schools join together to run prospect camps. Commonly a school will operate two or three camps each year. Stanford University has typically operated the largest and most well-known of such camps. Often more than forty colleges are represented on the field by both their head coaches and assistant coaches, from all over America. These coaches provide hands-on teaching to camp players in all aspects of baseball. Each player (and pitcher) is given an ample opportunity to demonstrate his skills in a variety of drills over the two or three days of camp. These players are then divided into teams where they play multiple round robin games against each other, all the while being both coached and evaluated by the coaching staff. Players typically receive a written assessment of their abilities, both strengths and weaknesses. And these assessments are designed specifically for the position your son plays. Then all of the coaches in attendance at these prospect camps will then share their information on every camper.

In addition to receiving top-flight instruction in every aspect of the game, the opportunity to speak with all levels of college coaches, as well as the opportunity to test one's abilities against other top players, these camps guarantee one key element. that neither travel team nor showcase events can provide. Both you and your son will know precisely who's watching him play. Each school will tell you which other schools and coaches will be attending their prospect camps. This kind of certainty has changed the face of college recruiting for young players.

Coach Todd Schiffnauer, at the time head coach at Dusquene University commented:

> "The days of showing up at games and tournaments, to see if there is any talent there, are over. Now we hold prospect camps."

And if your son doesn't see his favorite school listed on the Boston College, University of Virginia or Harvard Camp lists, you need only contact any of your son's preferred schools to find out which camps they will be attending. Then register your son for one of these dates

Club teams and tournaments still provide a very useful way for your son to develop his skills. But if you and he are particularly interested in his being seen by certain schools, prospect camps should be given your serious considerations.

Velocity Thresholds

Every reputable pitching coach will tell you that both location and ball movement are more important than velocity. Although this is true, your son should be aware that at every level of play, a pitcher must reach a velocity threshold if he is to be successful. And when it comes to being recruited by a college baseball team, achieving the velocity threshold for this level of play is very important.

Velocity threshold is simply an indicator which reflects the minimum velocity level that your son must have in order to compete at any given level of play. For example, if your son is competing in a house league environment, the demands for velocity will be much less than if he is competing for a job on an all-star or club team. So if he wishes to play at the highest level of play, you must adjust to these circumstances when determining when he should begin a velocity building program (i.e. long toss) and how intensive it should be.

For example, as a rule of thumb, if your son wishes one day to play Division I college baseball, the accepted velocity threshold for this caliber of play is a fastball of at least 80 mph. Most Division I pitchers throw considerably harder than this. But superior location and ball movement can influence a coach, provided that the player meets this 80 mph threshold. So when deciding at what age your son should intensify his velocity building program, you may wish to utilize this number as a barometer for him to be aiming towards. Because no matter how accurate and lively your son's pitches may be, he won't be recruited to play at the Division I level with a fastball in the mid-seventies.

Parental Participation

Parents have a huge role to play in the development and success of their child's baseball career. But this word *career* is not used in the sense of meaning that one has played at some professional level. If your son plays baseball for only two or three years, but has fun doing it, and along the way he also learns something about this game and makes some friends, then his *baseball career* has been a great success!

Enthusiasm and Support

As a parent you can help your son by providing him with tools that he can rely upon as he tries to build a strong playing foundation. Parents need to offer *enthusiasm* for their son's efforts. Like getting *good at anything*, it takes a lot of time, effort and patience. Particularly when so many of these drills and exercises, can become tedious with so many repetitions. But your *enthusiasm and support* for his efforts can provide him the energy to persevere. Especially when his efforts don't meet with immediate success. And often this will be the case.

His skills will take time to build, but it's easy to get down on oneself and sometimes, kids will find it convenient to just give up. But the expression of your enthusiasm and encouragement of his efforts can provide him the backbone he will need to stay with something. And when he does, it's bound to provide him all kinds of happiness and success down the road.

Understanding and Compassion

Besides enthusiasm and support, at some point, he's probably going to also need your understanding and compassion. A gung-ho expression of enthusiasm to go out and do the best that he can, or to continue to plug away at those tedious and often lonely drills, can be very useful. But this isn't what he'll need when things aren't going his way or when he's tired or worn out. In fact, a sound talking-to about that *stiff upper lip* approach and just continue to *barrel through it*, is exactly what he doesn't need.

Some days he's going to be *lit up* by a team. Everyone is. Even the best major league pitchers have their off days. So your job will now be a little more low key. Your role will be to offer your understanding and insights for him. Just to let him know that he's not alone and this happens to everybody. Or that some practices just aren't working out. So the best thing for him to do is to just walk away. Perhaps even take a few days away from the game. Your *understanding and compassion* in circumstances like this will prove invaluable to his continued growth. To say nothing of the relief it will provide him in making things feel just a little bit more like fun.

FUN

Remember that stuff – fun? That's what got him interested in the game in the first place. And yes, it is only just a *game*. None of this should be life and death for him, or you. I occasionally remind players that I work with, and the occasional parent in the stands, that nobody gets a shoe deal at the end of the season.

Baseball is a game that's supposed to be fun for everyone. It's easy for the players to sometimes get caught up in the desire to *win* the game. Sometimes parents get even more caught up in it than their kids. Winning is, after all, the goal of every game that I'm aware of. But it doesn't have to be the only goal, nor indeed even the most important one.

I've always found it instructive to hear former professional athletes talk about what they miss most about their careers. Whether you read the exploits of Micky Mantle, Joe Montana, John McEnroe, Gordie Howe or just about any other athlete—large or small—they all talk about missing *one thing*. None of them say that they miss *winning* the World Series, the national tennis championship or the division titles. Instead they all miss just one thing: *competing*!

So take a cue from all of these great players from so many sports, do what you can to help your son compete as best he can. And encourage him to take the time to enjoy this competition and learn from it, win or lose. Because he won't always have that opportunity, no matter how good he becomes. Time eventually takes it away from all of us. Just do your best to ensure that he too can one day look back at his baseball career with good memories and perhaps a smile.

The Overbearing Parent

It's pretty well guaranteed that any parent who becomes involved in helping his son improve his baseball skills, other than just showing up at the games to cheer for him, will soon be *criticized* by other parents. This prediction doesn't apply to just the sport of baseball. Any parent who acts as a receiver to develop his son's football passing skills, takes a few shots on his goalie son, or rebounds his son's three-point shots is bound to be criticized for an excess of involvement in his child's life.

Often it is said that this parent is pushing his son too much or that he's encouraging his son, for his own reasons. Some will even say that this parent is "living vicariously" through his son's successes. If not these specific comments, one is assured of hearing any number of similar opinions. And all will be critical of your excessive involvement in his playing.

And yet it's curious how these comments only arise when it comes to playing sports. Because similar opinions *aren't* expressed about the parent who regularly helps his son through his homework, which results in his scholastic success. Similarly, if his son plays piano, or excels in high school acting performances, or the band, or the church choir, or even school politics; it's perfectly understandable to do what we can to assist our child in these endeavors. It's even perfectly understandable if a parent takes pride in his child's achievements and his hard work. This kind of parent is viewed as conscientious, diligent, and is someone who is just being a *good parent*. But when the activity is a sport, for some reason this parent, who is simply trying to be there for his son, is now viewed as doing it only for himself.

There's not much that can be done in these circumstances other than to be patient and just endure. So long as you know that your son wants and needs your help, then you're doing the right thing. The remarks of other parents will just have to be ignored.

How Do You Know?

Often kids who start out gung ho about a sport lose interest over time. This isn't unusual and shouldn't be seen as a direct consequence of your involvement. Other sports, friends, girls, and jobs are all common reasons why kids drift away from a game they once loved.

But how will you know when perhaps you are part of the reason he's drifting away from the game? When does his training schedule become too much like work and not enough fun? How will you know if some day he's no longer playing for himself but rather, for you? The key is in being honest with yourself, and knowing what to look for in him.

Talk to Him

The easiest and most straightforward approach is just to talk to him and see how he feels. Jeremy has repeatedly told me that there are two times that he hates every year: the middle of October and the middle of January. Until recently, this is when Jeremy has closed down for the season and when he starts up again for the next year. Both at the end and the beginning of the season, I ask Jeremy if he really wants to play baseball. I tell him that he shouldn't play for me and reassure him that I would have plenty of things to do with my time, if he decided he didn't want to play. He hates these times of the year.

Be Watchful

There are a number of things you might look for, and questions you should ask yourself.

- Does he act like he wants to play?
- Does he act like he's interested in being around the game?
- Does he look like he's having fun?
- What's his energy level like when he plays or practices?
- Does he ask about future practices or games?
- Does he make suggestions about his practice schedule or drills?

- Does he practice on his own or only when you take him to the field?
- Does he talk about the games, practices, or his future with baseball?
- Is there exuberance in good performances and some disappointment when he plays poorly?
- Do you sense indifference?

There is no one sure-fire way to tell if your son still wants to play ball. Some kids are pretty outgoing and straightforward, so this child probably won't leave any doubt, one way or the other, about whether or not he wants to play baseball. But the more shy or reserved child shouldn't be mistaken for someone lacking enthusiasm for the game. They simply have a quieter disposition but may nevertheless still have a love for the game. Asking yourself the questions listed above and certainly asking your son how serious he wants to train are just a few of the ways that you may periodically review his interest in the game. Reminding him that you're only there for him and that he doesn't need to play for you should always be made clear. And if he still wants to play, then I hope that the ideas contained in this book can be of some help.

RECOMMENDED READING

The Mental Game of Baseball, H.A. Dorfman, Karl Kuehl
The ABC's of Pitching, H.A. Dorfman
Coaching Children in Sport, Martin Lee
The Cheers and Tears A Healthy Alternative to the Dark Side of Sports Today, Shane Murphy
Straight Talk About Children and Sport, Janet Leblanc
The Sport Psych Handbook, Shane Murphy
Positive Coaching Building Character and Self-Esteem Through Sports, Jim Thompson
So, You Want Your Kid to be a Sports Superstar, Ken Paul Misik
Play Baseball the Ripken Way, Cal Ripken Jr. and Bill Ripken, Larry Burke